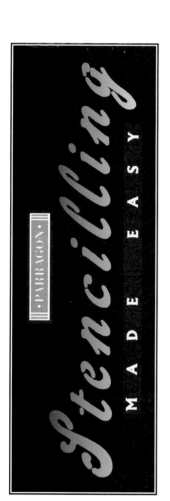

Stencilling

·PARRAGON·

MADE EASY

JOANNA SHEEN

First published in Great Britain in 1995 by
Parragon Book Service Ltd
Unit 13-17
Avonbridge Trading Estate
Atlantic Road
Avonmouth
Bristol BS11 9QD

Copyright © 1995 Parragon Book Service Ltd

ISBN: 0-7525-1087-8

Produced by Haldane Mason, London

Acknowledgements:
Art Direction: Ron Samuels
Editor: Lisa Dyer
Design: Paul Cooper
Photography: Joff Lee
Styling: John Lee Studios

Contents

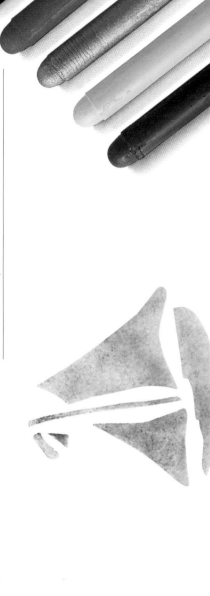

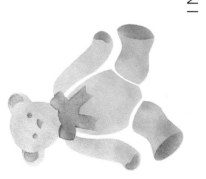

Introduction

Stencilling is an art form that can be handled by the youngest or least-skilled member of a family with great success. The very professional results that can be achieved with stencils belie the simplicity behind the technique; once you have mastered the first few simple strokes, it is plain sailing nearly all the way!

It is very unusual for any form of artistic decoration to result in near-perfect results from the very beginning, but it can be so with stencilling. The most difficult process is designing and cutting stencils. This being so, you may prefer to purchase ready-cut stencils from the extensive collections available and you will be certain to achieve wonderful results on your first project.

Once you progress to creating your own stencils, you will find inspiration all around you. A colour magazine accompanying the Sunday paper can provide great ideas for designs just as easily as a trip to an historic house or museum. Often a sheet of wrapping paper, wallpaper or even an advertisement in a magazine can be as inspirational as more complicated and beautiful images. Look for simple shapes that work well and experiment on lining paper or other scrap paper before you begin.

You will find many different ideas in this book. There are projects to show you how to stencil on a range of different surfaces, from terracotta and wood to fabric, paper and walls. Once you feel confident with the stencilling techniques, then many other ideas will occur to

you and stencilling will become a very useful and enjoyable craft skill to have and use.

The list of possible projects for stencilling is endless, as I am sure you will find once you have started. You can create beautiful decorations for your home or you can decorate or create your own greetings cards or wrapping paper, thereby adding your own personal touch and saving money too. Look for objects to decorate at flea markets and jumble sales. Furniture that appears to need some repair often needs only a good clean, a coat of paint and some fun with a stencil effect to create a beautiful piece of furniture that will be much admired. Read the basic techniques section (see pages 16–17) carefully before you start a project. Make sure you are happy with the basic ideas, never apply too much paint at once, always add a little more if it is too faint, take care and work slowly but surely, and you have a lot of fun ahead of you.

One word of warning! Once you have mastered the art of stencilling, then stencilling anything and everything soon becomes the order of the day! A successfully stencilled bedroom soon leads to the living room, kitchen and garage all being decorated with huge enthusiasm. Do remember it *is* possible to have a room left in the house that is not stencilled (I haven't!) when the urge to stencil comes upon you. I am sure you will have a lot of fun and satisfaction from this craft with a minimum amount of effort and investment.

A Brief History of Stencilling

Stencilling has been a popular craft and simple form of printing for centuries and the skill dates back as early as the second century AD. Japan and China have very fine stencilling traditions and many early examples exist of each country's art.

Chinese stencilling dates from about 600 AD, when pieces of leather, wood or vellum were used as the stencil rather than paper. Images were stencilled on cave walls, pieces of silk and leather armour. The image of a sitting Buddha is a popular one with early Chinese stencilling – and indeed it does make a good, simple motif if your project needs that theme in the design.

Japanese stencilling developed to decorate silk and fabrics for clothing and decorative purposes. The decoration on the garments would vary with the importance and social standing of the wearer, and a Samurai warrior's silk kimono would have much more elaborate and gilded decoration than a simple worker's costume, which may have had only a simple indigo stencil on cotton fabric. The Japanese refined their stencilling skills and continued to develop and improve their craft

long after similar traditions in other countries were being overtaken by the Industrial Revolution and the development of machine-printing.

Japanese stencils were not manufactured from wood or leather like the Chinese versions, but were made from a paper-like substance formed from the bark of a mulberry tree. The paper was made more supple by soaking it for some time in the juice of persimmons, a process which made the stencil waterproof and able to withstand more wear and tear. As the Japanese had developed their skills to such impressively high levels, their complex stencils were very different to the simpler designs used in other cultures. Their designs, or ties, to hold the stencil bridges, or ties, to hold the stencil together, were far less obvious and in many cases were non-existent. Where

we would expect to have a good solid 3 mm (⅛ in) of rigid card, they might have a few gossamer-thin silk threads or a fine mesh of silken threads, which gave their work even more detail and made the bridges virtually invisible once the design was printed. Today Japan still has a fine stencilling movement with many wonderful books on the subject being published and a good selection of paints and tools available.

European stencilling has its origin in Rome, where it was used as a rudimentary printing process in the second century AD. Later, the process became popular throughout many areas of Europe, including France and England. The materials needed to produce a stencil and the paints required were expensive and scarce, so most of the work was commissioned by people and institutions who could afford this form of decoration. As a result, early stencilling appears mostly on large buildings, such as manor-houses, churches and cathedrals. Simple repeat patterns were used to decorate walls, and more complex floral or animal designs were used to decorate paper and fabric.

Stencilled designs, either on paper or painted straight on to distempered walls, were a much cheaper method of reproducing the decorative fabric and tapestry that traditionally hung on walls. Hand-stencilled wallpaper would have been less than a quarter of the price of damask or cut velvet at the time. However, this popularity and economy led, in some ways, to the demise of hand-stencilled paper. As stencilling became more and more popular; so printing methods were developed to supersede the hand-finished versions and make decorative wallpaper even less expensive.

Gradually stencilling became used by all classes in society, and the decoration would appear in a relatively humble worker's cottage as well as in a beautiful palace. Stencilling also came back into vogue with the Art Nouveau movement at the end of the nineteenth century. In Britain, there is evidence that William Morris used stencils for wallpaper and ceilings, and many architects of the time, especially William Burges and, later, Charles Rennie Mackintosh, used stencils to great effect on furniture and interiors. Wonderful examples of British stencilling design can be found in museums, stately homes, churches and other historical buildings throughout the country.

A very strong tradition and history of stencilling also exists in America. Although wallpapers were imported from Europe and later manufactured in America, the cost was prohibitively high and beyond the means of the majority of the early settlers. Stencilling became an enormously popular and decorated walls, floors, fabric and furniture.

There are some wonderful designs dating from the nineteenth century, including repeat wall designs and also large single motifs using fruit, flowers and birds. These natural images of plants and animals were exceedingly popular in American decorative arts.

The colours used in early American stencilling are cruder than the more refined European pigments. Natural pigments were mixed into a paste with whey from the household milk supply. They had a mellow richness that was very different to the exotic colours being used in Europe at the time. Although many householders enjoyed stencilling their homes and fabrics, most of the work seems to have been done by a travelling band of craftsmen who would wander from town to town, offering their skills to the settlers and decorating walls or chairs, cupboards or chests, as required.

Much has been written about American patchwork quilts, but bedspreads were also decorated with beautiful stencil work. Stencilled decoration was also commonly used on furniture – mainly as an attempt to copy fine lacquer designs from the East. However, in my opinion, the finished results often surpass that which they were intended to copy. There are beautiful chests and cupboards, chairs and tables from the early American period, all finely decorated and many still quite exquisite. A good representation of these stencilled objects can be seen at museums, both in the United States and in Europe. They show that stencilling, despite being a craft all of us can enjoy, can produce special pieces that are truly remarkable when a really talented craftsperson executes the work.

Tools and Materials

One of the greatest bonuses of stencilling as a decorating medium is the moderate cost of materials needed to totally transform a room. In fact, once that initial investment is made, the cost would probably cover transforming an entire house, not just one room or object. The basic equipment you will need are brushes or other applicators for applying the colour, stencils, paints, and a pencil and ruler for planning the position of your design. If you intend to make your own stencils, you will

need additional materials, depending on the method you choose, as described below. Most of the tools and materials you will need are available from art and craft suppliers, from special stencilling and home-decorating shops, or in the craft section in department stores. Some specialist equipment is available from mail-order companies. Look in your phone book for specialist companies who will be able to help you find unusual items.

Brushes and other applicators

Some type of applicator will be necessary for applying the colour, and this will depend on your budget as well as your preferred method of working. Experimenting with various applicators before you start a project will help you decide which type works best for you.

It is essential to have a different applicator for each colour included in a project. So if you are planning a three- or four-colour design, then three or four brushes will be needed.

Synthetic sponges make the

least expensive applicators, but using them is not easier – just less expensive. Natural sponges can also be used, provided they have small holes. A sponge can be cut into several pieces, and each piece used for a different colour.

Sponge applicators are special

stencilling tools. They are very easy to control, allowing you to fill in tiny, detailed areas of the stencil.

Commercial stencilling brushes

are stubby brushes with short, stiff bristles. They make stencilling much easier and will give good professional results with the minimum of fuss and effort. The size of brush you will need depends upon the scale of your project. If you are using a large, relatively undetailed stencil and are decorating a wall or floor, then a larger size of brush, such as a size 6, is quicker and easier to handle. If you are tackling a smaller project or using more detailed stencils, then a more moderate size 4 brush is better. A size 2 brush is ideal if you are trying to capture some small details or using an intricate stencil.

Cleaning brushes and applicators

If you are using oil-based paints, some brush cleaner or white spirit (turpentine) will be needed for cleaning. If you are using fabric paints or emulsion (latex) paint, then warm water will clean the brushes adequately. Always read the instructions on the paint carefully so brushes or other applicators can be cleaned correctly in order to prolong their life.

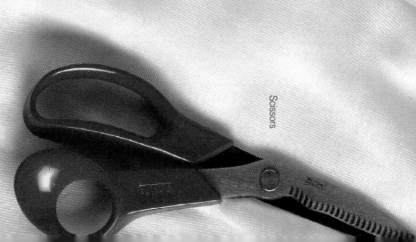

Scissors

Stencil-making equipment

As a beginner, it is far easier to buy plastic or card ready-made stencils (see page 14). But should you find that your enthusiasm leads you to making your own stencils, then another outlay of equipment becomes necessary.

There are two basic methods for making stencils. The first method (see page 12) is more difficult, but less expensive, and you will need a scalpel or craft knife, a cutting board or mat to protect surfaces, pencils and pens, tracing paper and stencil card. The second method (see pages 12–13) is a little more costly, but much easier to do well, and you will need an electric stencil cutter, a

sheet of glass and some opaque stencil plastic.

Stencil card is a specially treated paper produced by soaking manila paper in linseed oil, which makes it tough, waterproof and more like cardboard.

Stencil plastic is a transparent plastic sold in different thicknesses. A middle-range is best to use: if the plastic is too thick, it is difficult to cut, and if too thin it will bend too much.

Electric stencil cutters are available, at a moderate cost, by mail order or from some craft or home-decorating shops. The stencil cutter cuts through sheets of stencil plastic like a knife through butter, and fluid curves are immediately a success

because you 'trace' your design with the cutter.

Other useful supplies

Along with such items as kitchen paper and cloths to clean spills and protect surfaces, you will find it useful to have masking tape, a ruler, pencils, felt-tip pens, a chinagraph (wax) pencil, tracing paper and graph paper. A sheet of glass is not only necessary for cutting stencils with a stencil cutter, but it makes a useful palette for paints. You could also use an old plate or saucer, or small bowls or plastic containers.

Masking tape

Electric stencil cutter

Scalpel

Glass sheet

Natural sponge

Synthetic sponge

Ruler

Size 4 stencilling brush

Size 6 stencilling brush

Size 2 stencilling brush

Cotton buds (swabs)

Eraser

Paints

The type of paint you need depends heavily on the surface you are going to tackle (see page 11).

Emulsion (latex) paints can be used on many surfaces, but you will need to make a real effort at keeping the paint as dry as possible. You can buy the small tester pots of emulsion colours to use and these are available in a vast range of colours.

Oil-based stencilling sticks are a moderate investment initially, but are extremely long-lasting and have a wide range of applications. These paint sticks, or crayons, are excellent for use on all matt-finished walls, whether flat or wood-chip finish, and are versatile enough to use on other matt

surfaces, such as terracotta, painted or stained wood, and even fabric if you are not concerned about a long-term washable finish. With these paints, subtle variations in colour are simple to achieve using light or variable pressure. A wide selection of colours is available.

Fabric paints are essential for decorating any fabric project where you would like to be able to wash the finished item. The paints are available in a smaller range of colours than the stencilling sticks, and it is not easy to create lighter or darker shades just by using variations of pressure when applying the colour. However, the paints are still very enjoyable to use and widen the field of household items you can decorate considerably. The designs will not,

however, last indefinitely, and limited washing is probably the best option.

Water-based ink stamping pads are simple to use and perfect for paper-based projects. They are excellent for stencilling, as the ink pads are very dry and the range of colours is wide.

Aerosol spray paints produce some of the most beautiful stencil effects, but they do take some time and practice to perfect. It is all too easy to overspray an area or to accidentally spray a part of the design that should have been covered. Masking off areas outside the stencil may be necessary, as spray paints tend to spread. Also, be sure to work in a well-ventilated area.

Other paints are also available, and you could use acrylics, watercolours, gouache or metallic paints, or any other form of colour

Water-based ink stamping pads

Oil-based stencilling sticks

Choosing and using colour

You do not initially need a large palette of colours to begin stencilling. You might like to choose the exact colours you need for your first project, and then gradually build up a collection, or else start with a reasonable range of useful basic colours. When choosing the colour scheme for your project, think carefully about the base or background colour. Paler colours are effective on a pale cream or white wall, while a dark wooden background will need a much stronger colour for the design to register. Terracotta will soak up colour and needs strong amounts of very pale or strong colour for the design to show up well.

Emulsion (latex) paint tends to look similar in the container to the finished effect on the wall. This is not the case with the oil-based stencilling sticks. In many cases, these look almost black in the stick, but may be a strong blue, green or purple when applied. A dark blue can be applied very lightly to give a paler blue effect.

Gold and silver are available in fabric paints, oil-based paints and powders. A touch of gold always adds glamour, and all the metallic shades look attractive on their own or mixed with basic colours.

Although you can mix colours on a glass palette (like the one used throughout this book), using a single colour is much easier. Paints can also be mixed directly on the design (see page 17). All paints can dry out quickly. If you buy small pots of paints, then simply replace the lid. With paint sticks, use a resealable plastic bag for each stick of colour.

Preparing surfaces

If you are uncertain how your paint will react to a specific surface, it is a good idea to paint a small sample on an inconspicuous area first. All surfaces should be clean, dry, and dust- and grease-free.

Surfaces painted with a matt emulsion (latex) paint are the best for most stencilling projects. Even a textured wallpaper can be stencilled on if it has been painted with a matt emulsion. Avoid gloss finishes because the paint will not absorb. A painted surface that is peeling, whether plaster or wood, will need to be stripped down or sanded and repainted to provide a smooth, clean surface. If you are stencilling on a fabric, you will need to make sure the fabric is preshrunk and colour-fast. Natural fabrics are best to use, and avoid any glazed fabrics.

RIGHT From the top: natural wood surface, heavy paper or card (board) surface, calico (muslin) fabric, terracotta tile.

that appeals to you. Ceramic paints can be used for decorating plates and tiles, but as they will not have the durability of kiln-fired ceramic, care should be taken with how you use and where you place the object.

Varnishes

Your colour must be fixed (set) carefully with a varnish so the design will not wear off. Use an artist's fixative, matt or gloss aerosol spray varnish, or paint a coat of varnish on top of your design. Sealing with varnish is especially important for walls in areas of heavy traffic, or if you are decorating the seat of a chair or a surface that will receive a lot of wear and tear.

Fabric paints

Cutting Out a Stencil

There are two methods that can be used to produce a stencil: the first uses stencil card and a craft knife or scalpel, and the second uses an electric stencil cutter with stencil plastic. Both methods are possible, but the second is a lot less work than the other. Cutting through the card stencil with a scalpel can be hard work, because cutting curves with a straight blade is not always as easy as it looks. Both methods are described here, though, as you may wish to use both at some time or another. Refer to page 9 for the materials you will need.

Both begin with an original pattern or template to trace, such as those available from craft magazines or books.

Using clear or semi-opaque plastic for projects, as opposed to the buff stencil card, is another major benefit. If you are using a stencil cut from card, you cannot see the background on to which you are stencilling – if you are stencilling a border of a repetitive design, then being able to see what you have already stencilled or where the edges of the wall are positioned makes life easier!

Enlarging and reducing

If the design that inspires you is a little too large or too small, then it can be increased or decreased in size by photocopying the template.

Alternatively, you can size your picture up or down by using squared graph paper, and this method is perfect for enlarging or reducing the size of templates, patterns or simple line drawings (for more on sourcing templates, see page 15). To enlarge or reduce the size of a template, place a sheet of gridded tracing paper over the picture and trace the design.

Then copy the design, square by square, on to a larger grid for an enlarged size or a smaller grid for a smaller size.

Cutting a stencil from card

First you need to trace your design from the original template to the stencilling card. To trace the design, copy the template on to tracing paper with a pencil. Turn the traced design over, place on top of the card, and retrace to transfer the design to the card (the reverse side of the card will be the right side up). You could also use a sheet of carbon paper inserted between the tracing paper and the card to transfer the design. It is important to remember to leave a wide margin all around the design, of at least 7.5cm (3in), so when you apply the colour you will not brush paint on to other areas of the object.

Once your design is traced on the card, go over the design once again with a strong black felt-tip pen so it is clear and simple to cut out. You may find it easier to black out each piece to be cut out.

Work on a table with plenty of space so you can swivel your piece of card in all directions rather than moving your body. Protect your table with either a rubberized cutting mat, thick cardboard or thin wood. Always cut out the more delicate pieces of the design first, before tackling the large sweeps and curves.

Cutting a stencil from plastic

This method is far easier and no cutting mat is required because sharp tools will not be near the table. However, great care must be taken that the electric stencil cutter is switched on only when it is needed.

LEFT Place a suitably large piece of glass over your template. Tape the stencil plastic on to the glass or just hold it down with your free hand.

LEFT A chinagraph (wax) pencil can be used to trace the design on to the clear plastic before you cut it, but you may find it easier just to cut directly on to the plastic without following this step.

Begin by tracing the template, enlarging or reducing the image if necessary. Cut a piece of plastic the correct size for the design – remembering to leave a good 7.5 cm (3 in) border all around the design. Place a sheet of glass over your traced template, then cover the glass with the stencil plastic. Tape the plastic to the glass with masking tape, if necessary. I generally just hold the plastic in position with my left hand while using the cutter in my right. If you feel nervous about cutting directly on to the plastic, you can trace the design first with a chinagraph (wax) pencil.

Allow the stencil cutter to warm up for about 5 minutes. With an easy, even pressure, 'trace' over the stencil design with the stencil cutter,

problem with a piece of masking tape. Use a very small scrap on both the front and back of the stencil.

Cutting a multiple stencil

Often a design is simple enough to cut as just one stencil, but in other cases you may find it necessary to split the design into its various colour components. The main benefit from this is that you only need to paint one colour per stencil, rather than trying to manoeuvre around smaller details, remembering separate colours. If you want to split a stencil into separate colours, then just trace around the elements of the design

as though it were a pencil or felt-tip pen. Do not stay in one spot for too long or the cutter will melt an irregular patch from the plastic.

Once you have completed the cutting, place the stencil cutter in a safe place. With a gentle but sure movement, pull the stencil plastic away from the piece of glass. Where the stencil cutter has melted the plastic on to the glass, the plastic will adhere to the glass, leaving you a clean stencil to use. If this does not happen, then gently push through any loose pieces.

If you make a mistake when you are cutting the stencil by either method, then you can remedy the

RIGHT Allow approximately five minutes for the stencil cutter to reach the correct temperature. Using an even but moderate amount of pressure, 'trace' the design with the sharp tip of the cutter pressing into the plastic.

ABOVE Once you have finished cutting the design, gently but firmly pull the sheet away from the glass. Press out all the loose pieces that have not been left behind on the glass sheet, and your stencil is ready to use.

that need the first colour for your first stencil, and then do the same with separate stencil card or plastic for the second colour, and so on. Number and colour-code each stencil. Cutting small notches in two opposite corners through all the stencils will help you to line up the individual components to make the overall design. You can then pencil around the notches once the stencil is in position on the object, and use the pencil marks to register the next stencil.

Using Ready-made Stencils

Precut commercial stencils are available from a wide selection of outlets. Arts and crafts suppliers usually sell a diverse range, as do special home-decorating shops. Women's magazines often include features on stencilling, including actual stencils or templates to trace. However, the best source of ready-cut stencils is from one of the many mail-order companies (see suppliers on page 100), who offer a dazzling array of designs to give you inspiration and ideas for adding stencilling details to every conceivable place in the home. These

Professional stencils are nearly always sold on clear or opaque plastic for the same reasons that I recommend using clear plastic to cut your own stencils: the plastic allows you to see the work you have just completed and to keep to a continual line of work ahead of you.

Card stencils, such as the ones at the back of this book, are not as long-lasting as their more rigid plastic counterparts, but work perfectly well.

Ready-cut stencils can be taken at face value and used in exactly the way they were designed. It is also useful to consider separate pieces of the stencil. By masking off some of the details, you may be able to use just a ribbon or bow on its own, or pick out a single flower to repeat as a random motif. Some stencils are accompanied by ideas for different uses

LEFT Good, ready-cut stencils are an excellent investment, because they are long-wearing and designed by professionals. They are available in a huge range of designs.

ready-cut stencils have been designed by experienced stencilling professionals who have solved any problems with that particular design, and this makes them much easier for a beginner to use.

If you start your stencilling by using a commercial stencil, you have a very high chance of producing a splendid finished result first time around. Progressing to designing and cutting your own stencils is best done after you have become proficient at the actual paint and finishing techniques.

and these can mean very good value, as many different projects can be completed with only a few stencils. But equally good value can be obtained by purchasing your designs carefully and reusing various parts of the stencil.

Storing and cleaning stencils

If you have collected quite a few stencils, then keep them stored in a clean, dry way as cleanly and carefully as you can. An easy and efficient way to file them is to use large envelopes or folders, and to stencil a one-colour version of the design on to the front of each so you can see at a glance which stencil is inside.

Stencils must be cleaned immediately after you have finished with them. If you are using the oil-based sticks,

then a piece of clean kitchen paper is usually sufficient. If you are using emulsion (latex) or a similar water-soluble paint, then wash the stencil (if it is plastic) before storing it away.

BELOW To adapt ready-made stencils to your own designs, choose the section of the stencil you want to keep and mask off all other areas of your stencil with strips of masking tape on both sides.

Creating Your Own Stencils

Although there is a plethora of ready-made designs and stencils available in the marketplace, there may be several reasons why you prefer to create your own designs. Obviously, there is the cost element, as it is much less expensive to produce your own stencils than to buy someone else's ideas, but also there may be a more aesthetic reason. Perhaps you have always fancied a flight of hot-air balloons ascending into the spare bedroom ceiling or a flock of sheep galloping across the nursery walls and simply can not find a suitable stencil pattern in any of the commercial catalogues. Creating your own design is then the answer.

Inspirations and ideas can be gleaned from many places: newspaper colour supplements,

ABOVE A simple car motif for a boy's bedroom is found in an advertisement. Place the glass sheet over the car photograph.

magazines and papers, books, textile designs and advertisements, to name but a few. Any picture or design you find can simply be traced at the same size. If the design that inspires you is a little too large or too small, then it can be increased or decreased in size by photocopying or you can re-size your picture using graph paper (see page 12). Tracing actual objects can be one of the easiest ways to find suitable designs for your stencils. For example, pressed leaves can be drawn around or traced to help you create a leafy autumnal effect, or doilies can be used as stencils to give a pretty, lacy design.

If you have an attractive curtain, you could trace a small part of the fabric design to create a coordinating border or random design on the

ABOVE Cover the glass with a suitable piece of stencil plastic and, using an electric stencil cutter, trace around the shape of the car. Remember to include bridges to hold the stencil together.

walls. Children's books are also a great source for nursery ideas.

You must remember that for a stencil design to work, there must be legs or bridges to support the stencil. The bridges should be at least 3 mm (⅛ in) wide.

Examine your design and look for suitable places to insert the bridges. If the bridges of your stencil become too weak, false supports can be put in with neat strips of masking tape. All stencil designs need to be bold and flowing; practice is definitely the name of the game. Once your pattern is traced, follow the instructions for cutting a stencil from card or plastic on pages 12 and 13.

Basic Techniques

Stencilling is merely a method of directing where the paint is applied, and the way you use your stencil can be as varied as the patterns and colours of your projects. The very first step with all sten-cilling projects is to prepare the surface of the item you want to dec-orate (see page 11) and make sure all the materials you will need are easily at hand (see pages 8–11).

Planning your design

If you are creating a continuous border or repeated pattern in a line, it is a good idea to draw a thin pencil line along the base of where the stencil will rest. The pencil marks can be rubbed out later, and the line will

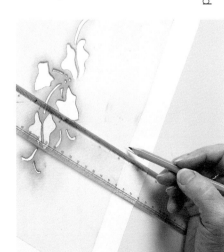

help keep the design straight and even. A random pattern usually only needs a good eye and constant checks that the designs are evenly spaced out. You may like to trace the entire design lightly on to the surface, especially if you are working with fabrics and other materials where there is no chance for correcting mistakes or where exact spacing is required.

Positioning your stencil

You may want to attach your stencil to the wall or surface you are decorating – although in some cases it is just as easy to hold the stencil with your free hand. Attach the stencil with several small pieces of masking tape. This tape is fairly good-natured and, if removed carefully, does not take paint off a wall or surface. Another alternative is to spray some spray adhesive on to the back of the stencil; the adhesive will make the stencil tacky and you will be able to reposition it five or six

times. Personally, I find spray adhesive sticky and messy, and it has once damaged the paintwork on a wall I was decorating. If you do use the adhesive, test it first on an inconspicuous area of the wall or object you are decorating.

Applying the colour

Once you are happy with your method of securing the stencil, you are ready to apply the paint. Make sure all your colours are easily available, preferably on a glass palette. The most popular applicator is the stencilling brush. The brush is used in an upright manner, and the paint gently applied with a slight circular movement. You could choose to use a stippling method with the brush or work around the edges first with a circular movement leaving the centre areas white. If you use a sponge, the paint can be dabbed on in short punchy movements to achieve a slightly patchy effect, which looks wonderfully rustic and antique.

ABOVE To position a stencil on a curved surface, tape the stencil in place with masking tape. You will need to use a reasonable amount of pressure to hold the stencil flat while you are applying paint.

ABOVE If you want your stencil design to be centred, first find the centre of your object. If you are working on a flat, square object, make sure all the angles are right angles and measure and mark an exact centre point on all four sides. Lightly mark a pencil line from top to bottom and side to side to connect the points. You can then position your stencil over the cross.

Dab any excess paint off the brush or sponge first and apply the paint as drily as possible, starting with the lightest colour first. The paint is best applied lightly, and if you wish

Basic Techniques

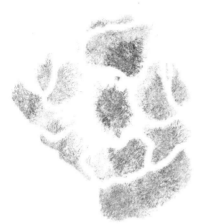

to strengthen the colour, another ccat can be applied to the same area. Repeating an application of paint to enhance the colour is far preferable to putting the paint on too thickly in the first place. After you have applied the first colour, remove the stencil and check the density of colour. If you are not happy with the result, replace the stencil and gently add a little more paint.

Allow the first colour to dry completely before repeating with the remaining series of colours, and check the back of your stencil occasionally to make sure it is clean.

Many of the media you choose to use can be mixed by painting one colour over another. A dark centre in the middle of a flower can be created by using the lighter colour first and then adding the darker colour later. Always apply the lighter colour first; this way you will get two clearly defined shades. If you try to apply the darker paint first, the two shades blend and are indistinguishable.

Finishing your design

After the last coat of paint is dry, fix (set) your design by using an artist's fixative or varnish (see page 11). For hard-wearing surfaces, you may need to apply several coats of varnish. If you are in any doubt as to which sealant or varnish is best for the paints you are using and the object you are stencilling, read the manufacturer's recommendations included with the paints. With fabric

paints, follow the manufacturer's instructions included; usually pressing the fabric is the correct way to fix the colours.

Random pattern

Here a simple duck stencil has been applied at random without any preconceived ideas of placement. A random composition eliminates the need for measuring.

Ordered pattern

Here the duck motif has been used in a formal, ordered composition. All small motifs can be used in a variety of ways to make stripes, borders, diagonals and squares. Some planning is usually needed because it is essential not to run out of space before you have completed a full design.

Stippling

A stippled paint effect is achieved by loading a stencilling brush fairly heavily with paint and holding it upright, then dabbing on to the stencil until the area to be covered is completely painted.

Circular-motion stencil brush

This flower has been painted using a size 4 standard stencilling brush. The brush is moved in a circular motion which gives depth and intensity to the colour, and can produce lighter or heavier shading.

Sponged effect

This sponged paint effect is produced using a small, dry natural sponge with oil-based stencilling sticks. The sponge is rubbed into the paint and then dabbed over the area to be stencilled and an airy, textured finish is the result. The centre of the flower has been sponged a second time with some brown to add a little shading.

Edging

Here an edging effect is achieved by using a standard stencilling brush and a minimal amount of paint. The brush is moved in a circular motion, but only around the edge of the flower and then a tiny amount of coverage in the middle. This effect is easier to achieve on a larger image and looks especially striking when the background colour is strong.

17

Projects

These projects are simple to do and stunning in effect. Just follow the steps and you will find it easy to transform an ugly old chest into a magical children's toy-box, or bare white walls into a beautiful bower of roses. All the ideas are designed to inspire you to try creating your own stencils, designs and colour combinations, as well as helping you to practise the basic skills of stencilling.

Teddy Bear Time

Painting Charming Designs on Nursery Walls

One of the many good points about stencilling is the moderate cost involved. When a new baby is imminent and there are so many other demands on the budget, a stencilled design in the nursery can achieve a lovely effect with minimal expense. When planning your stencil for a nursery or small child's room, keep the design simple and uncluttered. The choice of colour is obviously a personal one, but often primary colours are more popular with children. A soft dreamy colour scheme that you find irresistible may be rejected by a 'discerning' two-year-old who would much prefer a design in bright fire-engine red with a touch of emerald green and banana yellow thrown in for good measure!

If you want to create your own designs for children's walls, there are many interesting and attractive ideas suitable for children. You could plan your design around a favourite cartoon or storybook character, or use a general theme, such as transport, the circus or farm animals. The fabrics you have chosen for the room often provide good inspiration for a stencil design, and an image can be traced from curtains or bed linen. With a new baby you obviously have a free hand, so whatever theme delights you is a possibility. Hot-air balloons

fading into the distance, fluffy lambs, alphabet letters or tractors all make charming designs.

There are many precut stencils available that are specially designed for children, and these would be ideal if you do not feel comfortable with cutting out stencils. You could also combine one of your own designs with a ready-made stencil, by adding a balloon motif to a precut teddy bear stencil, for example.

Plan your decorating scheme carefully before you start work. First of all, decide on a random pattern, an ordered composition, or a combination of the two. One possibility would involve a carefully measured border of regimented toy soldiers at the height of a picture rail or as a divider between two colours or types of wallpaper. Another idea would be to use a border design at one height with a random design making a wallpaper effect above or beneath the border.

When you have decided on your decoration and have prepared your surface (see page 11), lightly mark the walls with crosses or lines in pencil so you obtain the effect you want with the correct spacing or randomness. It will be too late to correct the design after you have stencilled it in the wrong position!

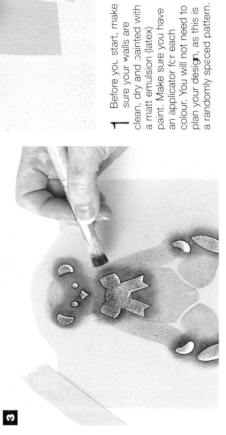

2

1

3

Materials

- Teddy bear and duck stencils (see Stencil Templates, page 103)
- Masking tape
- Oil-based stencilling sticks in red, orange and blue, or colours of your choice
- Size 4 stencilling brushes
- Glass palette
- Satin or matt aerosol spray varnish

1 Before you start, make sure your walls are clean, dry and painted with a matt emulsion (latex) paint. Make sure you have an applicator for each colour. You will not need to plan your design, as this is a randomly spaced pattern.

2 Begin with the teddy bears' bodies, arms and legs, and apply the first colour lightly, painting another coat to darken if necessary. Paint the bears randomly around the room, leaving enough space to add the ducks and bricks.

3 Add a contrasting colour for the bear's paws and bow, such as the blue used here, taking care to position the stencil accurately so the bow is in the correct place and does not cover the bear's face. Add the paws and bows.

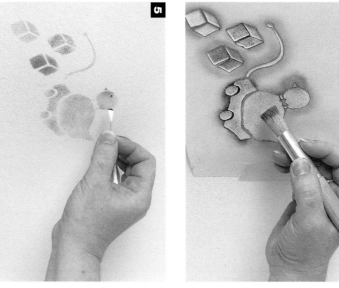

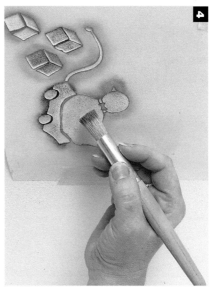

4 Next add the stencil design for the duck on wheels and bricks. Use several colours on this stencil, with one colour for the duck and two or three more for the bricks and wagon. Accuracy is important and you may prefer to use a size 2 stencilling brush rather than a size 4 brush.

5 Using a cotton bud (swab), rub the end into a little of the blue paint or another colour if you prefer. Gently dab the cotton bud in the correct position on the duck to create an eye. Repeat for all the eyes.

BELOW So many different colourways are possible for this design, from pastels to vivid hues. Bright colours may be more appealing for young children, but you must also take into account the overall colour scheme of the room and the fact that, with luck, your work will last for many years.

6 Once you are happy with the finished paintwork and the entire project has been completed, spray the design with varnish. Choose satin or matt varnish, because gloss varnish is too heavy for an emulsion (latex) paint base.

OPPOSITE This charming design adds a delicate softness to a nursery wall and is suitable for either a boy's or girl's room.

22

Wild Roses

Using Trailing Patterns on Bedroom Walls

T here are many shapes and sizes to use in stencil decoration, and the rose design chosen here illustrates a free-form pattern that can be adapted as you progress. Some thought is needed beforehand to plan the spread and location of your design, but exact measurements are not necessary. If you feel really unsure about committing a stencilled rose to the wall without prior sketching or planning, then you could stencil a few of the large roses on to lining paper and lightly tape them in position to give you a rough idea of the number and general size of the decoration you want. Although this rose design has been suggested as a bedroom decoration, any wall can be decorated in this manner. The roses could make just as attractive a scheme in a hallway or main living area as in a bedroom.

When you are using a solid, geometrical pattern or a straight repeat design, it becomes crucial that you get the measuring and repeat spacing perfect or the images that are just a little too far apart will catch your eye forever! However, with most floral designs you can easily add a twig, tendril, spray of leaves or a few buds – whatever blends with the overall design – to extend or fill in a basic composition. This is particularly useful should you feel there is an empty

for stencilling. Bright colours and vivid patterns show up well against a pale background, as do soft pastels. If you find white too stark, try a magnolia or buttermilk colour to add warmth. A dark background can be very effective when stencilled with gold or silver paint, such as in a night sky scheme with stars and moons or gold fleur-de-lis against a bottle-green background. White and other very light colours also show up moderately well on dark backgrounds, but I would still advise caution because dark colours are more difficult to paint over.

patch that you would like to fill or a design you would like to twist around a corner. A lovely flowing bough of willow or sprays of spring catkins are so easy to add to and twist by adding an extra branch here and there!

There are many different textures and surfaces of walls that can be stencilled, depending on the type of paint you use (see page 10). If you are using the oil-based stencil sticks, as shown here, then make sure the surface is painted with a matt rather than a gloss paint, or that your wallpaper is matt and does not have a glossy finish.

A wall painted with a pale colour is usually the easiest and most successful

Materials

- Rose stencils
- Oil-based stencilling sticks in reds and greens, or colours of your choice
- Size 2, 4 and 6 stencilling brushes
- Glass palette
- Satin or matt aerosol spray varnish

1 Before starting, make sure your walls are prepared and you have a brush for each colour you will use. This design is intended to be halfway between a random design and a carefully placed frieze. The roses tumble down the wall and can be added into the design freehand.

2 Paint the leaves first to establish the size and range of the design, leaving space for the flowers.

3 Add some roses into the design, using a pale red and concentrating on the outer part of the flower. The darker middle will be added later. All the roses can be the same colour or you could mix various shades.

4 Using a darker red, shade in the centre of the flower and shade some of the edges of the petals to give extra interest to the design and some variation in the overall colour.

5 Add extra leaves to pad out the design where you feel there is too large a gap. Leaves are always useful fillers as they are unstructured, particularly in this type of design, and they can always be used to add a little extra colour here and there.

6 Once you have finished the design and are happy with it, spray the design with varnish. This will help give the paintwork a longer life and help it resist knocks and scratches.

OPPOSITE Trailing roses look beautiful in rooms. You may like to continue the effect down to the floor at the corners of the room.

Helpful Tips
● A size 6 stencilling brush is essential for larger designs on walls, like the roses here. If you try to use a smaller brush, you will get a very patchy effect. Large brushes are also useful for stencilling floors.

LEFT When you are considering which colour scheme to use, it is not necessary to stick rigidly to natural or lifelike colours. Here, the roses have been coloured blue and the effect is just as attractive. Exploring unconventional possibilities makes the number of choices limitless.

BELOW When you are redecorating a room with a new theme, such as these roses, the idea can be carried through with complementary stencils to decorate other parts of the room, like drawers or curtain tie-backs.

BELOW You can use a stencil like this one for a trailing project, combined with various other components from other stencils, each used singly. Alternatively, you can make or buy a stencil with more detail on each piece, so only one or two stencils need to be used.

Iris by the Stream

Stencilling on Bathroom Walls and Tiles

Bathrooms can be ideal candidates for stencil effects, as they are usually fairly small rooms and there will be less area to stencil than with a large living space. Most people spend a limited amount of time in the bathroom, so it is fun to create a really striking design that has a lot of impact when you enter the room. Elaborate or overpowering designs are not well suited for large rooms in which you are going to spend much greater amounts of time because you may tire of the effect very quickly!

I have always felt the need to decorate bathrooms with a vaguely watery theme, such as water lilies, shells, ponds, or seaside or river bank scenes. This is not necessary, though, and no doubt there are many designs that would look stunning in your bathroom that do not have even a remote connection with anything vaguely wet or watery.

A design on the ceiling of a bathroom can be very effective. However, I can not recommend an easy way to apply the paint – it is definitely a two-person job or, alternatively, use the same method as Michelangelo with the Sistine Chapel and lie on scaffolding!

Walls covered with ceramic tiles can also be decorated with small random designs or even one large design. Use ceramic paints for dec-

look to your existing bathroom decor. For example, if you have old-fashioned coloured tiles on the floor, repeat those colours in a striking geometric pattern used as a wall border or on a mirror frame.

As with all surfaces to be stencilled with oil-based sticks, the walls must be clean, grease-free and completely dry before you start work. The stencilled decoration will stand up to the steam and heat of bathrooms very happily, provided that you have started from a good, clean base and that you liberally apply several coats of varnish over the top of your work.

orating tiles, but do not expect the painted tiles to have the same hard-wearing nature as fired tiles. So if your bathroom is heavily used, and particularly if you have young children who may inadvertently scratch the tiles, then you may have to retouch or paint over the design when deterioration sets in. A special ceramic sealant is useful to varnish the tiles after decorating, but you could also use a standard varnish.

You may also like to stencil bathroom accessories to match your overall theme. For example, a shell motif used on the walls could be repeated on a mirror frame, linen basket or chest of drawers, perhaps in another size. Alternatively,

Materials

Materials
- Iris stencils (see Stencil Templates, page 103)
- Masking tape
- Oil-based stencilling sticks in brown, green, blue and purple, or colours of your choice
- Size 2, 4 and 6 stencilling brushes
- Glass palette
- Satin or matt aerosol spray varnish

1 Make sure your walls are clean, dry and painted with a matt finish. You will need a suitably sized brush for each colour you intend to use.

2 This design is intended to be a more regular pattern, and must therefore be measured carefully. Plan how many flowers you can fit in the space, so you achieve a well-ordered design and avoid any uncomfortable spaces.

3 Begin with some leaves to form the basis for the design. Place them regularly along the top of the wall to be decorated, so you have space to repeat the pattern later. Alternatively, you can place them randomly and fill in with extra leaves at the end.

4 Next add the flowers, using a lighter colour on the outside of the flower so darker shading can be added later. Add all the flowers of one type at the same time to keep the balance and ensure that there are not too many of one type of flower.

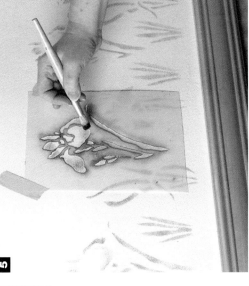

5 Now add the second, larger iris stencil to create a more prominent effect to the overall design. Again, use a paler colour to the outside of the flowers so they can be shaded later.

29

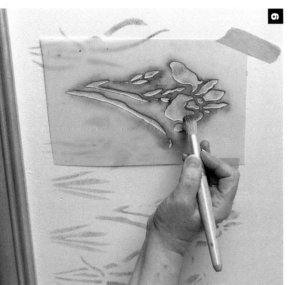

ABOVE There are many possible colour options, whether one uses natural colour schemes or not. In this case, both these optional colourways are fairly lifelike, but a strong colour scheme in black and silver, or red and orange, could look equally effective in another setting.

6 Here, a darker shading is added to the centre of the flowers. This can be a darker tone of the same colour, or a contrasting shade to highlight the flowers.

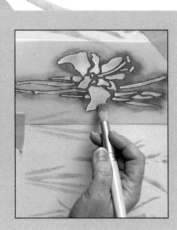

An alternative way of obtaining a contrast in the flower's centre is to allow the colour of the wall to show through. In this case, a white wall gives a pale highlight; however, using a coloured wall could be really striking.

7 As a finishing touch, fill in any gaps with extra leaves or add a humorous touch, like these bees. Bees or butterflies make very useful extras to fill unwanted spaces in designs with floral or country themes. Paint them using several different colours that tone with the overall design.

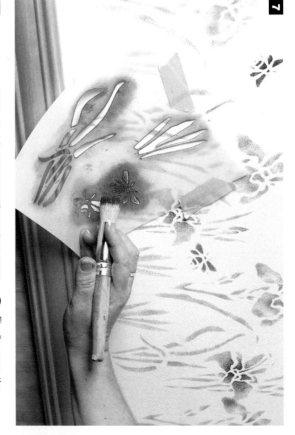

8 Finally, spray the design with varnish to protect it against knocks and scratches. This is particularly important when designs are lower down on a wall. When they are positioned higher up, they are unlikely to get damaged, but at this level the design needs extra protection.

OPPOSITE The irises pick up the colours in both the wallpaper and the rail to make a highly complementary design.

Strawberry Fields

Decorating a Child's Chest of Drawers

Pieces of furniture are wonderful objects to decorate, as their appearance can be dramatically altered and adapted to a particular decor. Although a child's chest of drawers has been chosen for this project, you could use any other similar object you like. Even the most plain and inexpensive item can look elegant, countrified or ultra-modern, depending on the paint effect you choose. Many pieces of furniture can be purchased at a very low cost from junk shops, jumble sales or from family members. With a few hours of work, a lot of elbow grease and a little flair, you can turn a dull piece of furniture into the focal point of a room.

Many different styles of furniture are suitable for stencilled decoration, and looking for suitable pieces can become an enjoyable hobby in itself. The first criteria when choosing a piece to decorate is obviously whether there is a flat area free for decoration. Take careful note of the spaces between handles or other raised decoration, as this impedes the free flow of designs and more planning and measuring will be necessary. Often a simple, basic piece can be the perfect candidate for stencilling, as other three-dimensional decorations, such as elaborate mouldings, do not intrude.

Once you have decided upon the piece you wish to decorate, whether it is old or new, you must make sure that the surfaces are all smooth and painted the colour that you want for your background (see page 11). If your furniture is an old second-hand piece, then you may need to strip off the old paint, sand down the surface, and stain or paint the wood. Otherwise, you may just need to clean and repaint the item before decorating it. When painting prior to stencilling, always leave lots of time for the paint to dry. If you stencil too soon after painting, the design may blister or lift off.

After you have planned the decoration details and carried out the stencilling, you must finish the painted areas with several good coats of varnish. I always use a spray varnish, as its easy handling ensures that no smudging or running of the paint occurs. Repeated coats of varnish are particularly essential on a piece that would receive a fair amount of wear and tear, such as a dining-room chair or kitchen cupboard. Pieces like the chest of drawers pictured here would obviously receive a reasonable amount of use around the handle area, but the sides of the chest might need fewer coats of varnish. The choice of varnish finish is really a matter of personal preference.

Materials
- Natural wood chest of drawers
- Strawberry stencils (see Stencil Templates, page 103)
- Oil-based stencilling sticks in red, green and blue, or colours of your choice
- Size 2 stencilling brushes
- Glass palette
- Satin or matt aerosol spray varnish

1 Make sure your piece of furniture is properly prepared for stencilling. A natural unfinished wood chest was used here, but you could also use one that has been painted with an emulsion (latex) paint. You will need enough brushes for each colour, and you will need to plan the placement of your decoration.

2 Paint the green leaves on to the longer drawers using the full stencil. You can either paint the stencil centrally between the two handles or extend the decoration the entire length of the drawer.

3 Paint the leaves on to the smaller drawers at the top of the chest. Either cut a stencil in half or mask off some of the leaves (see page 14), so that you do not smudge any green paint where it is not required.

4 Add the red strawberries on to the drawer fronts. Although red automatically comes to mind when using a well-known fruit like strawberries, the design can look equally effective if you use dark purple, as if the berries were blackberries, or a mixture of white and red to look like unripe strawberries.

5 Paint some small design using a contrasting colour, like the blue chosen here, so they show up well against the wood. Other accents could be added, such as small bees or birds.

RIGHT The design can be as simple or as complex as you like, and you can increase the amount of stencilling by adding extra berries or more butterflies.

5

6 When the entire chest is finished, spray the decorated drawer fronts liberally with varnish to protect the painted area against any wear it may be subjected to.

6

BELOW Other colourways can all look equally stunning, but bear in mind the colour of your background. If you are painting on stained wood, use a strong colour that will contrast well. Lighter pastels would show up well against a pale-coloured painted chest.

Helpful Tips
● When using tiny stencils like the strawberry ones here, use size 2 stencilling brushes. If you try to use a larger brush with such a small stencil, you may slip and cover areas you wanted to keep clear.

OPPOSITE These sweet little strawberries add a fresh country feel to a child's chest of drawers. For a more rustic look, use a wheat and flower stencil.

Ribbon Garland

Applying Pretty Detailing to a Dressing Table

Pretty stencilled images can turn a plain or utilitarian piece of furniture into a real delight. This dressing table has a mirror which makes careful planning necessary, but the design is easy-to-execute and takes very little time to do; the resulting effect makes the table look so much more attractive than when it was plain white.

To plan a theme in a bedroom, or any room, use a colour or pattern from one of your already-existing interior decorations for inspiration. For example, use a blue ribbon or a floral motif from the bed linen as your design and repeat it throughout the room, with decorative touches here and there to match. If there are plain lampshades beside the bed, then a ribbon or flower could be stencilled on them to match your walls, or you could stencil the design on a bedspread or pillows. Matching cushions can also be decorated and placed on a nearby chair, and wide mirror or picture frames also lend themselves well to decoration. I am not suggesting that all these bedroom elements should be decorated, but a small selection of them will tie the colour scheme together well.

To prepare the surface of your piece of furniture for stencilling, see pages 11 and 32. Take great care when stencilling small, narrow

piece of furniture with a colour that contrasts with your background colour, such as a Wedgewood blue if your base is white or cream. When the paint has dried, carefully remove the cut-outs and you will have an ivy leaf design, but with white on blue rather than the reverse. This technique can be achieved by using natural products too, such as pressed leaves and flowers.

To improve the longevity of your painted decoration, you can of course spray with varnish. However, another good idea is to protect the top of the dressing table with a sheet of glass.

or difficult-to-reach spaces on your furniture. You will need a very small detailed stencil, which may be tricky to place in position and may not look as effective as you intend. If you have a small area that you feel needs a touch of colour, then you may find it better to settle for a single leaf or tiny bow to match or complement your design, rather than trying to repeat a scaled-down version of your whole design.

To try an alternative method of decorating to the one shown here, use reverse stencilling. To do this, attach cardboard cut-outs of a simple motif, such as ivy leaves, in a pattern on the areas you wish to decorate. Then spray-paint the entire

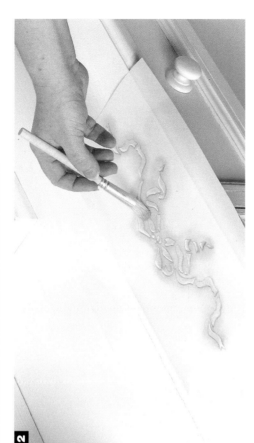

1 Before you start, make sure your dressing table is prepared for stencilling. You will need enough brushes for each colour you will use, and you will need to measure and mark where you want to place the stencils, keeping balance in mind.

Materials

- Dressing table, painted in white emulsion (latex)
- Ribbon and bow, ivy and floral stencils (see Stencil Templates, page 103)
- Oil-based stencilling sticks in pink, green and blue, or colours of your choice
- Size 2 stencilling brushes
- Glass palette
- Satin or matt aerosol spray varnish

Helpful Tips

● Always clean brushes immediately after use with a suitable cleaner. Leaving them overnight or longer will make the task many times harder than immediately rinsing them in white (mineral) spirit or water.

2 Begin by stencilling the top surface. The ribbons can be stencilled in one colour only, such as the pink here, or darker shading can be added to the streamers or central knot.

3 Paint in the ivy leaves in green. These leaves can also be shaded with a slightly darker colour. Small tendrils and berries can be added to give extra length to the design, or a few single extra leaves can be used to fill in odd corners or parts of the object that cannot take the entire length of the stencil.

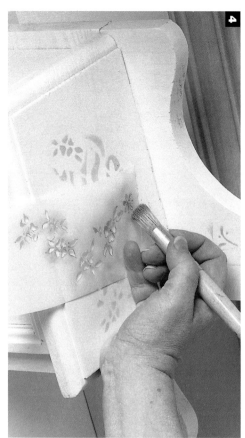

4 Add small flowery details around the ribbons in blue. Using several different colours for these smaller flowers would also look stunning, but you will need a steady hand and tiny brushes to keep the colours from running together and blending.

LEFT Ivy is an ideal motif to use as a stencil because it is a trailing plant and can have leaves added or taken away without affecting its appearance. This gives you complete flexibility when decorating difficult areas that have limited room for manoeuvring.

5 Once the design is finished, spray all the painted areas really well with the varnish to protect the surface. If you wish, the top surface of the dressing table could be covered with a sheet of glass to shield the paint effect from damage.

Individual ivy leaves have been added to the bow and smaller flower designs to give a bolder, heavier decoration to the corners of the dressing table top. Make sure that the treatment you give one corner is repeated on other corners so you achieve an appropriate symmetry.

OPPOSITE A plain, white dressing table becomes an exquisite piece of furniture with a little stencilling. The soft colours accentuate the elegant woodwork.

Rabbits and Balloons

Adding Fun Features to a Child's Toy Box

A large wooden chest or toy box makes a wonderful blank canvas on which to create a fantastic stencilled effect. You can use either one really large design that will cover the top and possibly the sides of the box or, as in this project, a collection of smaller designs to give a random decorative effect.

Using a collection of different stencils can be a fun way to decorate a plain toy box. If the child is interested in dogs or cats, then a selection of various breeds and colours make a lovely display. Likewise, a selection of train engines and associated images would please a railway enthusiast. An effective design can be created by tracing large block capitals from newspaper headlines to make your stencils, and covering the box with gaily-coloured letters randomly placed all over the surfaces – some touching each other and others a little way apart. An even more simple decoration could be achieved with large and small spots. To do this, make stencils in various sizes of circles by tracing around the bases of cups or small bowls, then stencil brightly coloured or pastel dots all over the toy box. Another similar idea is to make stencils of simple shapes, such as squares, circles, diamonds, stars and hearts, and use these to decorate the toy box.

of subtle colours that can be achieved by using lighter or heavier pressure is highly effective. You may prefer to use other paints, such as the small tester pots of emulsion (latex) paint, but they do not produce the same shaded look. For a bright, fun approach, use gouache paints in vivid or metallic colours. Do remember with any project that is going to be heavily used, particularly by children, to apply several coats of varnish over the design. If your painted box does become damaged, you can retouch the paint or even plan a new decoration if the old design becomes too battered and worn to save.

Old chests, trunks and boxes can be found fairly inexpensively at flea markets and junk shops. You will need to prepare the surface well (see pages 11 and 32). Remember to clean and paint the inside thoroughly, especially if the box is to be used for storing toys, linen or other objects. Covering the inside with some lining paper is a good idea for those containers that are to be used as linen chests, as the paper can be replaced as often as you like. For a more decorative effect, line the inside of the box with fabric, gluing the fabric in place along all the edges.

I find the oil-based sticks the best paint for this type of project. The range

Rabbits and Balloons

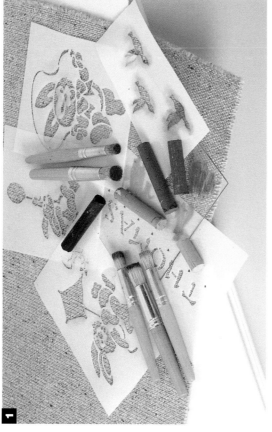

Materials

- Wooden toy box, painted in cream emulsion (latex)
- Selection of rabbit and alphabet or name stencils
- Oil-based stencilling sticks in yellow, green, blue and red, or colours of your choice
- Size 2 and 4 stencilling brushes
- Glass palette
- Satin or matt aerosol spray varnish

1 Make sure your box is prepared for stencilling. You will need suitably sized brushes for each colour, and you will need to make a rough plan of where you want to place the stencils.

Helpful Tips

● To find suitable letters for a stencil of a name, use the headlines from the newspapers. Cut out the letters required and paste them on to a sheet of rigid card and then cut the stencil out (see pages 12–13). If you have a computer, you could also use or adapt a font to create an individualized template – just print out your work at the appropriate size, or enlarge it by photocopying, and cut the stencil! Alternatively, buy a stencil that gives you the entire alphabet.

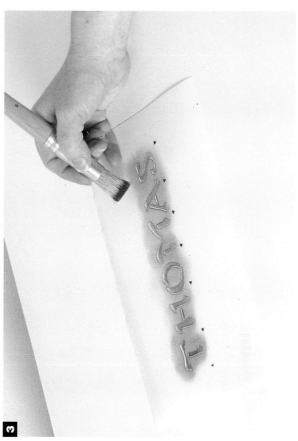

3 Paint in the name first, using a bold colour that will show up well, such as the red chosen here. Alternatively, paint each letter of the name in a different colour, but if you do this, use a small brush to help you keep the colours separate.

2 If you are planning to add your child's name to the top of the box, you must measure accurately to ensure that the name is exactly central and level (see page 16). Or, place the name off-centre to the bottom left or in another position that does not require such precise planning.

41

ABOVE When you are stencilling rabbits or other motifs on to the side of a box, you may find it easier to lightly tape the stencil on to the box with masking tape. This will hold it in position and free up your left hand.

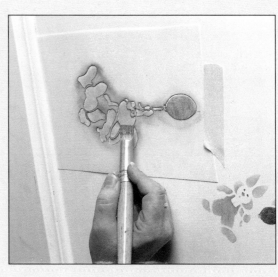

Helpful Tips

● Once you have made a template of the letters in your child's name, this could be reduced or enlarged on a photocopier to use on other projects, such as lunch-boxes, school satchels, or shoe bags.

5 Once you have covered the toy box with your decoration, spray the entire box with at least one coat of varnish, but preferably two. An item like a toy box will receive very rough treatment and the more protection you can give your handiwork the better!

4 Paint in the rabbits randomly all over the box, using a variety of different stencils and colours. A further selection of animals, such as a collection of zoo or circus animals, would also look attractive and fun.

OPPOSITE Happy little rabbits in different shapes and sizes brighten up this toy box, but you could use any other animal or motif you like.

Creeping Periwinkle

Personalizing a Design for a Child's Chair

Children greatly enjoy personalized designs and gifts. They feel very strongly about their name, as indeed we all do, so decorating an object with a child's name usually gets enthusiastic reactions. The letters used can either be bought as precut stencils or can be made up into a stencil by tracing newspaper or magazine headlines.

Where you place your ornamentation and the theme you use will obviously vary with the type of chair you are decorating. If you are stencilling a chair with little or no decorative woodwork on the back, then you have more scope for design work than on the chair shown in this project, where the back can only take minimal decoration. To stencil a name on the back of the chair, either the front or back side, you will first need to measure and mark the position of the letters, centring the name carefully.

As with other objects that may have awkward areas to stencil, a floral design is often easier to use on a chair (see page 24). If you choose a precise geometric pattern, you will have to plan and measure your design carefully to make sure it fits the chair exactly.

Look for chairs in junk shops or flea markets. Chairs that are discarded by one person can often be joyfully rescued by another, and

other type of chair, such as wooden folding chairs, kitchen chairs or dining-room chairs.

For an alternative version of the project here, stencil a design on to one of the 'director's' chairs that replicate the type of chair a Hollywood director uses. These chairs are available in adult and child sizes, and are constructed from a wooden frame slung with canvas. You will need to use fabric paint to stencil on to the canvas, but the results look extremely effective and the decorated chair would make a wonderful gift.

you may be lucky enough to find a suitable piece that has been left for garbage collection. Any type of chair, including metal chairs, is worth considering, and you would be surprised at the effects possible with a rejected chair, a little paint and a stencil or two.

Completely sanding and refinishing a second-hand chair is important. Metal chairs can be sprayed with a matt-finish metal paint, and wooden chairs can be stained or painted. Both finishes look attractive, but you should take your other furniture and interior decoration into consideration. The same basic steps for decorating the child's rocking chair in this project can be used to decorate any

Creeping Periwinkle

Materials
● Child's rocking chair, painted in white emulsion (latex)
● Selection of floral stencils, including a name stencil
● Oil-based stencilling sticks in light blue, dark blue and green, or colours of your choice
● Size 2 stencilling brushes
● Glass palette
● Satin or matt aerosol spray varnish

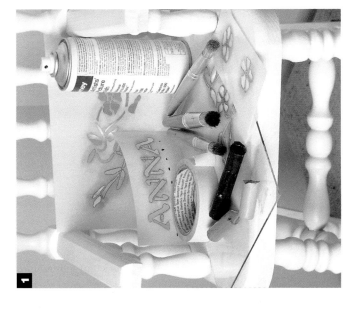

1 Before you start, make sure your chair is prepared for stencilling. You will need enough brushes for each colour you intend to use. Plan where you want to place the stencils, particularly the name stencil, and make light pencil marks in the correct positions.

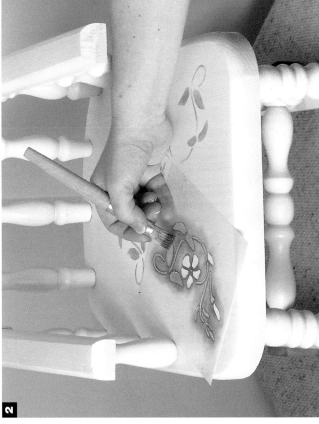

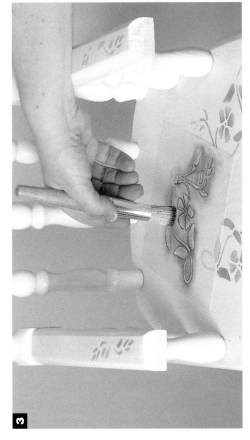

2 Start with the seat of the chair and paint a twisting rail of green leaves around the seat. How heavily you decorate the chair is up to you – you might like to paint the edge of the seat and the chair legs as well.

3 Add some periwinkle flowers to the spray of leaves that you have painted on to the seat. The flowers can be all the same colour, as demonstrated here, or a gaily coloured mixture of shades to make the finished effect brighter.

45

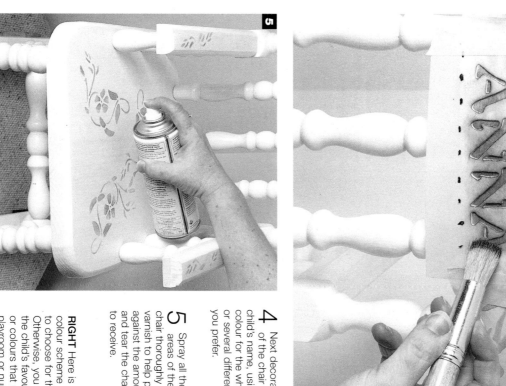

4 Next decorate the back of the chair with the child's name, using one colour for the whole name or several different colours if you prefer.

5 Spray all the decorated areas of the rocking chair thoroughly with varnish to help protect against the amount of wear and tear the chair is bound to receive.

RIGHT Here is another colour scheme you may like to choose for this project. Otherwise, you could use the child's favourite colours or colours that match the playroom or nursery where the chair will be placed.

RIGHT The seat of the rocking chair will obviously receive a great amount of rubbing and wear, so you may like to add a second or third coat of varnish after you have finished your stencilling.

LEFT Children love to see their name on their belongings. If you want to add further details, such as a date of birth, then the name could be painted on to the front of the chair and a date of birth added to the back.

OPPOSITE Flower stencils look charming on rocking chairs for little girls. You might like to adapt the design for a boy by using nautical themes, which are softly attractive yet definitely masculine.

Garden Ivy

Revamping Old Wooden Trays

T he project here uses a set of wooden trays, which could easily be found among odds and ends at auctions and antique markets. Other types of trays could also be used; for example, an inexpensive metal tray could be painted with a matt-finish spray paint or a matt metal paint and then stencilled. Many people have old trays that they rarely use because they are a little scratched and worn, and these could be repainted and given a new lease of life.

Several good base coats of paint are of paramount importance. If the tray is a dark colour and you are painting it a light colour, then more coats may be needed to cover the old colour or pattern. Once the base coats have been painted and the surface is sufficiently smooth (you may have to sand it down lightly), you are ready to begin stencilling.

Trays must be able to withstand spills, as they are most commonly used to carry beverages, so make sure you choose a suitably protective varnish to coat your finished design. Carefully varnish the entire tray at least two or three times. You may also like to cover the bottom of the trays with baize or felt to prevent the trays from scratching table surfaces.

Flowers, leaves and garden themes are easy design choices for trays, as they provide an attractive multi-purpose decoration. However, if you have a special colour scheme or theme in your kitchen (or the room in which you will use the trays the most), then this can be repeated on the trays. Another possibility is to trace a motif from the china that you would use regularly on the tray on to a stencil. If, for example, you have a pretty rose design on your teapot or china mugs, then use the rose pattern as the basis for your stencil design, adding a few leaves and stems to extend and embellish the design.

You could also decorate the trays with random repeated patterns, such as a simple triangle in various sizes, a teapot shape in different colours, or the word 'TEA' in various lettering styles. A flower-bed design could be positioned so one long side of the tray acted as the flower-bed, with various plants rising towards the top of the other long side, and a butterfly or bee floating in the 'sky'. You may also like to make a matching cloth for the tray, repeating the same stencil decoration or a small motif from the whole design. To do this, use a plain cotton cloth and fabric paints, and follow the instructions for the Kitchen Flowers on pages 88-90.

Garden Ivy

LEFT Here, the ivy design is painted in red and brown to give a completely different effect. You might like to first experiment with different colours and shading on heavy paper or on a surface similar to the tray; this will allow you to create your own unique colour scheme.

3

1

1 Make sure you have enough brushes in suitable sizes for each colour. Decide whether you are going to use the same motif or different ones for all your trays, and then prepare your trays for stencilling.

Materials
- Wooden trays, painted in a pale emulsion (latex)
- Ivy stencils (see Stencil Templates, page 103)
- Oil-based stencilling sticks in a range of greens and blue, or colours of your choice
- Size 2 and 4 stencilling brushes
- Glass palette
- Satin or matt aerosol spray varnish

2

2 Begin by painting on the trails of ivy using a pale green paint. A darker green colour will be added as shading later on.

3 Once you feel you have enough ivy leaves around the tray, use the shading stencil to add a darker green tinge to the leaves in the middle and on some of the edges. You could also add some dark brown or reddish shading, if you prefer.

4 Add some more detail to the design with sprays of berries and stems. These are painted here in green, but they could just as easily be black or brown to give added contrast.

Helpful Tips
● For trays and other objects that will need to be wiped, you could spray them with a single, thorough coat of varnish and then, when the first coat is dry, paint a second coat of a more substantial varnish on to the surface with a brush.

5 Finally, paint in some blue butterflies. These add a feeling of lightness and pretty detailing to the design.

6 Once the trays are decorated, spray them very thoroughly with several coats of varnish. As they will be well used, they need a really good coating of varnish to protect your artwork.

OPPOSITE These delightful ivy-covered trays turn an afternoon tea in the garden into a really special occasion.

Terracotta Hearts

Painting Flowerpots and Planters

Decorated flowerpots make very attractive gifts, with or without plants, and the plain terracotta plant pot is not expensive. You can choose from tiny pots for miniature plants to large planters. Some of the pots are sold with saucers to hold excess water, and these can be decorated to tie in with the design on the pot.

Oil-based stencil paints show up very well on unglazed terracotta. The only drawback is the depth of colour in terracotta, and a paler plaster flowerpot would give you a lot more scope for choosing colours. If you wish to use a terracotta pot, but do not want to include the deep terracotta colour in your colour scheme, simply paint the flowerpots with several base coats of a coloured emulsion (latex) paint. The effect can be very striking; for example, a selection of large cream-coloured planters with green frondy plant designs on them would look wonderful in a sun room or conservatory.

Large terracotta planters and containers that are to be used outside can also be decorated, but they will need some all-weather protection. Because painting varnish directly on to a design with a brush can cause the colours to smudge, I recommend using two coats of a

of decorated flowerpots, gardening accessories and seeds would make a fabulous gift for a keen gardener. A large wide-necked terracotta bowl could be decorated with a fruit or vegetable stencil, and then used to present a lovely collection of fruit or vegetables. Smaller pots can be gilded around the edges, stencilled with gold paint, and then filled with homemade chocolates, biscuits or cakes. The flowerpots can also be matched to your interior decoration; for example, if your kitchen is blue and white, you may like to decorate a white painted pot with blue motifs and use the pot for growing herbs.

spray varnish over the stencilled design first before covering the entire object with yacht varnish or another finish suitable for outdoor use. Fixing the design first with a spray varnish will prevent any smudges or smears occurring.

You can also decorate other terracotta objects, such as kitchen storage jars and crockery, in the same way as the flowerpots. If the objects are to be used in the kitchen, they should be varnished to protect the design against the damaging effects of grease and dust.

Decorated flowerpots can also be used to present other gifts. The pots can be filled with flowering plants or fresh or dried flower arrangements. A collection

Materials

- Plain terracotta pots in sizes of your choice
- Heart, star and bow stencils (see Stencil Templates, page 103)
- Oil-based stencilling sticks in red, blue and gold, or colours of your choice
- Size 2 and 4 stencilling brushes
- Glass palette
- Satin or matt aerosol spray varnish

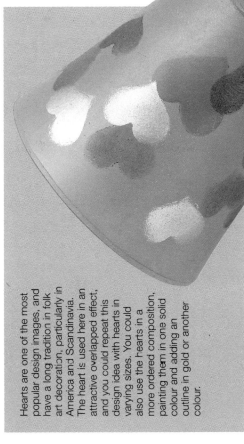

Hearts are one of the most popular design images, and have a long tradition in folk art decoration, particularly in America and Scandinavia. The heart is used here in an attractive overlapped effect, and you could repeat this design idea with hearts in varying sizes. You could also use the hearts in a more ordered composition, painting them in one solid colour and adding an outline in gold or another colour.

1 Using your first colour, and holding the stencil firmly with your left hand (or right hand if you are left-handed), paint a few hearts randomly on to the plain terracotta flowerpot. You will need to use quite a strong colour, like the red shown here, to counteract the orangey terracotta background.

2 Using the second colour, blue, and using the same heart stencil, add some more hearts to your pot, overlapping them on to the first hearts slightly. You may like to keep the heart motifs separate, or to create a band of hearts around the top and bottom of the flowerpot.

3 Using a third distinct colour, antique gold in this case, add some more hearts. Gold and silver both stand out against the terracotta background.

4 Give the flowerpot a good coat of spray varnish. If you want to make the design weatherproof for outdoor use, spray varnish the pot first and then paint several thicker coats of an outdoor varnish on top.

OPPOSITE Decorated terracotta pots can be used both indoors and out, and make individual, attractive and inexpensive gifts.

LEFT Here, a terracotta saucer has been decorated with a ring of gold. There is not enough space to decorate the saucer with stars to match the flowerpot, but the use of the gold colour links the two pieces together well.

LEFT A pretty purple ribbon adorns this flowerpot, and the pot would look attractive holding a plant in a bathroom or bedroom. The bow stencil is rather long and consequently a little trickier to hold in position while you are stencilling, so take a little more care than usual when applying the paint.

Fruit and Vegetables

Creating a Recipe Box File for the Kitchen

L ooking for unusual ideas for presents can be time-consuming, and this project would make a perfect gift for someone who loves to cook. The project uses a basic cardboard box without dividers or cards; the cards were later purchased from a stationery supplier. Paper-based products are very satisfying to decorate, as you can create a completely unique project for very little expense. You may want to extend this project to other forms of paper products, such as writing paper, notes or envelopes (see pages 68 and 72).

The box could be given with recipes included on the cards or the cards could be blank, depending on your enthusiasm at the time! If you are decorating a recipe box for yourself, then duplicating the project for another person is easy. Each divider could be decorated to illustrate different sections; for example, stencil a chicken on the poultry recipe section, a carrot on the vegetable section, or a cow or sheep on the meat section. Alternatively, you could just decorate each divider (or card, if you are feeling ambitious) with a simple leaf, flower or herb.

The box file does not have to be used as a recipe file. You could use it as a card index for business contacts and decorate it with a more

abstract pattern in stronger colours. The box could be used for indexing collectibles too; many of these items, such as antique cutlery or books, lend themselves to interesting decorative motifs.

The recipe box used here is covered with brown paper, so you can use a variety of different paints on the surface. Water-based ink stamping pads are a good choice, the oil-based stencil sticks, as used here, are very successful, and other watercolour or acrylic paints are suitable as well. Felt-tip pens can also be applied through a stencil if you like the effect they create, and these are ideal for children to use.

Remember that with a dark-coloured background as the base colour, you will need to use colours that are slightly brighter than if the background had been white or cream. Obviously, if you would prefer a lighter background, paint the box with several coats of emulsion (latex) paint in a colour of your choice. Make sure that when you are base-coating items for stencilling you use a matt-finish paint. Paint will not adhere properly to glossy finishes, unless you use special car spray paints which can be tricky to use. The box will be handled a fair bit, so finish with a coat of spray varnish to set the design and protect the paint against wear.

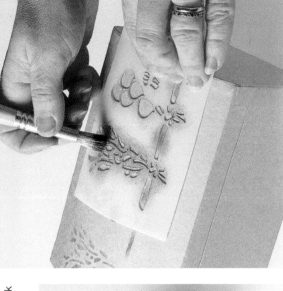

3 Stencil each bunch separately in a different colour to give a good contrast. To produce a shadow and add a little three-dimensional quality to the design, use a darker colour to shade the onions on one side.

4 Use a small brush to paint on the more intricate details, making sure that the area is completely covered and the colours are kept separate. Either paint the vegetables their authentic colour, or use a little artistic license to add alternative colours to the design.

Materials
- A card box and set of plain index cards
- Fruit and vegetable stencils (see Stencil Templates, page 102)
- Oil-based stencilling sticks in green, yellow, rown and red, or colours of your choice
- Size 2 stencilling brushes
- Glass palette
- Satin or matt aerosol spray varnish

1 Before you start, make sure you have enough brushes for each colour you intend to use. If the only boxes you can find are too brightly coloured or have an unsuitable surface, then you can cover them in brown paper or even a light-coloured handmade paper. Use plenty of glue to make sure that the paper is completely and evenly stuck down all over the box.

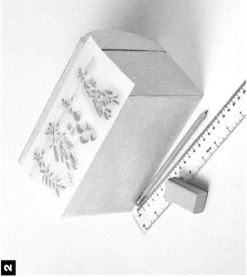

2 Plan your design so it fits exactly on to the sides and top of the recipe box file. To extend the stencil, you could add another bunch of vegetables, or you could remove a bunch to make the design smaller.

5 Next paint the tops of the bunches a leafy green. The design will look more striking if you choose bold, definite colours.

particularly if you are using a box with a brown finish, like the one here.

6 To add interest to the design, paint some details on each vegetable bunch, such as dots on the corn or veins on the onions. Repeat the whole process on the sides of the box.

7 Finally, spray the entire recipe box with varnish to protect it from knocks and spills in the kitchen.

OPPOSITE Fruit, herbs, vegetables and other kitcheny motifs transform a recipe box file and dividers.

BELOW Although realistic colours may seem the obvious choice for this project, purple carrots might brighten up the recipe box, or use a completely blue colour scheme to match a blue kitchen.

BOTTOM The divider cards inside the recipe box can also be decorated with single bunches of ingredients so they match the exterior of the box.

58

Ribbons and Tulips

Making a Beautiful Wooden Jewellery Box

Small boxes are fun to work on and very successful items to decorate. Boxes are available in many shapes and sizes, heart-shaped, round, square or tri-angular, and they can all look beautiful with some stencilled motifs added. They make excellent jewellery boxes, but also good gift boxes for other presents.

Boxes and containers to decorate can be obtained from many different sources. Although attractive containers can be bought, you can use simple cardboard boxes from previous gifts or even left-over packaging from food ingredients. Tin cans can be painted with enamel paints and glass jars given a base coat of emulsion (latex) paint. A large coffee jar, painted with several coats of matt emulsion, can be decorated with some very pretty stencil work to make an attractive container for the kitchen or bathroom. Light wooden round boxes, such as those used to package cheese, can be painted and decorated, and many other possibilities may occur to you as you look in your kitchen cupboard.

When choosing your box to decorate, remember that a flat surface is easiest to stencil on and curved or semi-circular lids or surfaces can be very much harder. Try to choose a container that is square, particularly if this is your first attempt at stencilling, or a box with a flat lid.

Any matt surface can be decorated, such as a painted cardboard box or a painted wooden surface, as with this project.

Planning your composition carefully is imperative, and you may want to trace your design lightly on to the box before you actually begin applying paint. Scale is an important factor to consider – the design should be planned so it fits neatly on to the box, leaving some space around the edges. Should you decide to decorate the box with a border design, then you must calculate carefully how the four corners will fit together. A decora-tive geometric border, such as small dia-monds set in squares, is not difficult to produce and you may find it best to mea-sure your box first and then alter your stencil to fit.

Small random motifs are usually the easiest way to add some dec-oration to a box and the random pattern will allow you to avoid prob-lems with corners matching. However, do not try to stencil a very tiny design; unless the stencil is beautifully and very meticulously cut, a well-defined and clear image is difficult to achieve. Remember also that boxes are made to be opened and the inside of the box can be stencilled to add interest. Even just a small motif on the inside of the lid is striking and unexpected.

1 Make sure the surface of your box is prepared and that you have the correct number of brushes for each colour you want to use. Plan your design, measuring and marking where you want to place your stencils.

2 Place the stencil in the appropriate position on the top of the box and start by stencilling the ribbons in blue. If you want to expand the design to fit a larger box, the ribbons can be elongated by adding extra tails or streamers.

1

Materials
- A plain wooden jewellery box, painted in pink emulsion (latex)
- Ribbon and Tulip stencils
- Oil-based stencilling sticks in red, green and blue, or colours of your choice
- Size 2 stencilling brushes
- Glass palette
- Satin or matt aerosol spray varnish

3 Next paint in the leaves and flowers. Choose colours, like the green and red here, that will give a good contrast to the ribbon; otherwise, the leaves and ribbons can become indistinguishable from each other.

3

2

4

6

4 Decorate the sides of the box. Use a different but complementary stencil, like the one here, or continue with the same stencil that you have used for the top of the box, perhaps masking off some of the design to use only a small part of the design to use only a whole stencil (see page 14).

6 Finally, when you have completed all the decoration, varnish the entire box well with the spray varnish. Cover both the inside and outside of the box. Leave the inside and top edges to dry before closing the lid, or the box will stick fast.

5 If desired, add a small design inside the lid. Here a stencil has been created that is very similar to the one on the lid, but it has only one tulip instead of several.

5

OPPOSITE A little treasure chest for jewels is easily created from a painted wooden box and a few simple stencils.

LEFT Here is the same stencil, but in a different colour. You can repaint your box any colour you choose to create a background that is sympathetic to your stencil design.

Paper Flowers

Customizing Office Supplies and Folders

Decorated files and stationery products make the office a prettier place to work or home-filing more fun. The standard files used in this project are available from large stationer's or office stationery suppliers. Try to select the plainest ones you can. Some files have heavy black printing across the flap, which spoils any stencilled designs, so look carefully before you choose your brand of file and make your selection according to the colour that suits your design best. Because painting the surface of the file is not possible, you will be limited to the colours available from your local supplier.

Decorating paper products means you can use a variety of paints, either water-based stamping inks, water-colour paints or the oil-based stencil sticks. You could also consider acrylics or other mediums. I prefer the water-based stamping inks, used in conjunction with the sponge applicators, or the oil-based sticks. As a precaution, spray the finished design with a light varnish, using either the standard variety or a special artist's fixative available from art and craft suppliers.

Decorating ordinary items, such as box files and folders, immediately makes them a possible gift item. If you are creating your own

homework or exam notes, and you could incorporate their names into the design, as well as images from their interests and hobbies. Another idea is to decorate the folder according to the contents; for example, a file for electricity bills could be decorated with light bulbs or a cookery recipe folder could be stencilled with fruit and vegetables. Once you are underway with a folder project, you will find it easy to repeat your designs on stationery; blank postcards or other notepaper. You could even use a special stencil as your own personal logo to decorate your headed stationery or letter-writing paper.

stencils, use your imagination and consider the person who will be receiving the object. For example, a box file decorated with flowers and flowerpots could be filled with seed packets and tips torn from gardening magazines, and this would please any avid gardening enthusiast. Father's Day presents could be solved by decorating a large file for home-office use, with motifs taken from his favourite sport or hobby. Sports cars and racing flags could decorate the file of a car enthusiast, and reels, spools and various sizes of fish could decorate the file of a fisherman.

Children may also be amused to receive personalized folders for their

Materials
- Assorted office folders
- Poppy stencils (see Stencils, page 103)
- Oil-based stencilling sticks in red, green, grey and brown, or colours of your choice
- Size 2 and 4 stencilling brushes
- Glass palette

1 Make sure you have a suitably sized brush for each colour you want to use. The composition is simple enough not to need any advance planning.

1

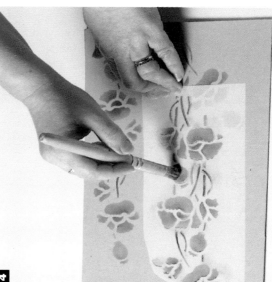

2 Position the stencil on the folder and paint in the stalks and leaves. Depending on your taste, you can either just decorate the flap for a more minimal design, or cover the entire folder for more profuse poppies.

2

3 Next stencil the poppies using a strong red colour. Shade a little towards the edges of the petals by applying more pressure to get a darker colouring.

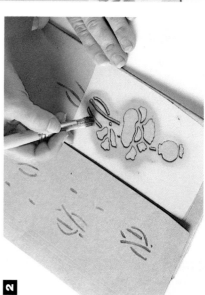

3

Helpful Tips
- As an alternative to oil-based stencil sticks, you could use the water-based ink stamping pads for this project. Apply the ink with sponges or sponge applicators.

4 Add the poppy heads in grey or brown, and also shade the centre of the poppies with the same colour. Adding shading gives more depth to the design and looks far more effective.

4

RIGHT A very strong design is created here using an iris stencil in strong pinks and mauves. A few bees have been added in a mauve colour and they help intensify the pretty colours in this decoration.

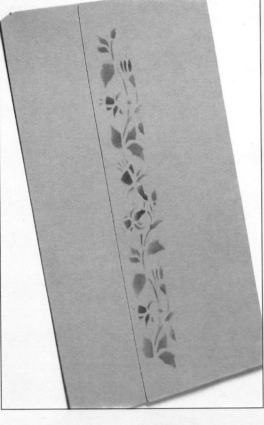

LEFT Here the folders have been decorated in a much more minimal fashion, with a neat line of fuchsias across the edge of the flap. If you are decorating a selection of folders, you may like to make some much bolder in both colour and composition than others.

ABOVE The same poppy stencil has been used here, but with different colours. The yellow colour scheme would be less successful on a darker background, such as pink folders.

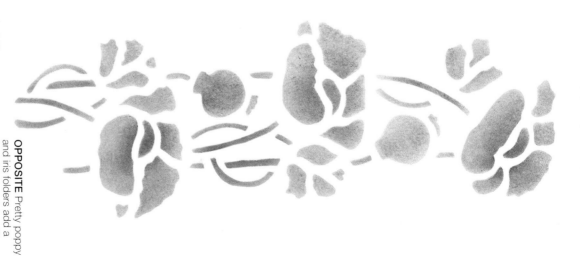

OPPOSITE Pretty poppy and iris folders add a feminine touch to office or personal organization, but you could adapt the idea by using any stencil you prefer. A border around the edges of the folders would also transform these ordinary items.

Purple Columbine

Making Wrapping Papers and Gift Tags

W rapping paper is always a great expense, especially at Christmas time when there are so many presents to wrap. The paper is usually ripped off the gifts and simply thrown away. Why then do we pay such vast sums for sheets and rolls of beautiful paper when a much prettier and more economical solution is right under our noses?

Brown paper or cream drawer lining paper is very well suited to stencilling and can work with ink stamping pads, watercolours, acrylics and stencilling sticks. The paper is available by the roll and works out relatively inexpensively. If you invest in a large roll, then suitably sized sheets can be torn off and used individually. Working this way allows for flexibility and gives you an opportunity to create different designs on each sheet as you need it.

If you are creating your own stencils for gift-wraps, there are many images you could use. Designs for children's wrapping papers could include traditional motifs, such as teddy bears, lambs, drums, cars or dolls, or more abstract patterns, such as squiggles or shapes in bright colours. For animal-lovers, choose cats, dogs, fish or wild animals, depending on personal tastes. Flowers are always a safe choice, as they are popular and appropriate for almost every occasion. If you

wrap. Although many festive stencils are commercially available, making your own is a fun project during the holiday season. Search through old Christmas cards for motifs to make up into stencils.

To make matching gift tags, cut a rectangle from the brown or cream paper and fold it in half. Stencil a small image on to one side and thread some ribbon or string through the corner to attach the tag to the gift. Take care to choose a small stencil when decorating the tag, or else reduce the size of your wrapping paper design to create a new, smaller stencil (see page 12).

are stencilling some sheets just for 'stock' supplies, so you have some paper handy when the need arises, then flowers are one of the best themes. Ivy, roses and honeysuckle images work well, but other suitable ideas include hearts, polka dots, and ribbons and bows.

A vast range of striking images are suitable for Christmas paper, such as holly and ivy, poinsettias, wreaths and angels. Stars and other simple shapes look highly effective when painted in gold and silver, and a Christmas tree is an easy image to trace when creating a stencil. Christmas trees could be stencilled all over the paper in shades of green and gold to produce a festive gift-green and gold to produce a festive gift-

P u r p l e   C o l u m b i n e

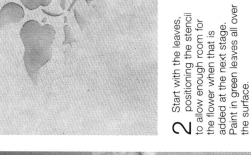

Materials
- Brown packing paper
- Green string or raffia
- Floral stencils (see Stencil Templates, page 103)
- Oil-based stencilling sticks in green and purple, or colours of your choice
- Size 2 and 4 stencilling brushes
- Glass palette

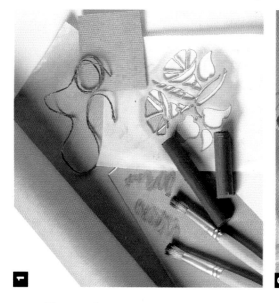

1 Make sure you have a brush for each colour. The easiest and often most effective way to create wrapping paper is to place the stencil randomly, so advance planning is not really necessary.

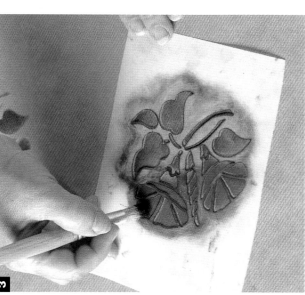

2 Start with the leaves, positioning the stencil to allow enough room for the flower when that is added at the next stage. Paint in green leaves all over the surface.

3 Paint in the flower using bold colours to counteract the dulling effect of the brown background. You can either use the same colour for all the flowers, or use several different colours to achieve a multi-coloured effect.

Helpful Tips
- As an alternative to brown wrapping paper, you could use cream or white drawer lining paper or any other inexpensive paper available. Of course, if you want really extravagant wrapping paper for a special occasion, choose among the many beautiful handmade and textured papers that are available from stationers and artist supply stores.

69

ABOVE Delicately coloured flowers make a perfect gift-wrap design for a Mother's Day present or a spring wedding gift.

OPPOSITE The natural motifs stencilled on these gifts look attractive against the rustic brown paper. For a more graphic effect, use more abstract designs on high-quality coloured paper.

4 Make a matching gift tag by carefully cutting out a rectangle of paper. Fold it in half to make a square and thread some string, raffia or thin decorative cord through the corner. You may like to trim the edges with wavy-edged scissors for more decorative effect. The tag can then be stencilled to match the wrapping paper.

RIGHT This technique can be used for all kinds of wrapping papers, from the stencilled Christmas tree and stars gift-wrap shown here to wrapping papers for birthdays, anniversaries, weddings, christenings, or any other celebration. Floral designs are particularly useful as they are suitable for myriad occasions.

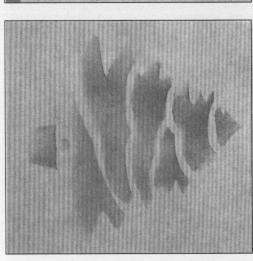

Helpful Hints

● An excellent time-saver is to wrap the gift first and then stencil the flowers straight on to the package in position. This allows you to place the motifs exactly where you want them. With this method you also avoid discarding those little decorated scraps that are often left over after gifts have been wrapped.

Creative Greetings

Designing Your Own Greetings Cards

H andmade stencilled greetings cards give a tremendous amount of pleasure to the recipient and they take a minimal amount of time to produce, especially when compared with painting or embroidery. The area where stencilling really comes into its own is on large numbers of identical designs. If you are designing and cutting a stencil for one card only, it can be a little time-consuming, but if you decide to create your own Christmas cards, for example, then a little time invested in planning your design and creating the stencil is soon repaid with the quick and simple production of a large number of cards.

Good quality card or heavyweight paper is important for handmade cards, as a card that bends and collapses when you try to stand it up immediately looks unprofessional. One stumbling block can often be finding an envelope the correct size. The easiest way around this problem is to buy envelopes first, then purchase your card or paper in the toning or contrasting colours that you require and cut the individual cards to fit the envelopes.

Once you have created a stencil, do keep it clean and safe in a clearly labelled folder. At some later date, even if you decide not to use the same stencil again, a part of that design, such as a small bow,

from stationers, and are excellent for this purpose, as they are very dry and come in a wide range of colours. They can be applied with sponges, small brushes or even with cotton wool buds (swabs).

Finally, when planning your designs, remember that stencilling can be used together with other ideas. For example, a bouquet of flowers could be stencilled on to a card and a satin ribbon bow added to give three-dimensional interest. Paper cut-outs, silk flowers, children's erasers and small sweets can all become part of an individual card.

leaf or flower, may be just what you need to fill a space on another project!

Numbers and letters are often useful for greetings cards. A special birthday or anniversary can be commemorated with a card bearing a large 25 or 21. Large letters and numbers can be sourced from newspapers and magazines, making it very simple to personalize a card with a name, number or date.

Care should be taken with the choice of paints. If you try using watercolour or other water-soluble paints, they should be kept very dry or smudges and smears may spoil the design. Pads of stamping ink have been used on all the cards shown here. They are easily available

Materials
- Envelopes and pieces of rigid card or heavyweight paper, in colours of your choice
- Ink stamping pads, in a selection of colours
- Sponge applicators or small pieces of sponge
- Cotton buds (swabs)
- Various stencils

1 Choose the correct size of envelope, cut a piece of rigid card and fold it to fit. Plan the design before cutting the stencil. Have several applicators or sponges to hand, using a different applicator for each colour.

2 Before making any marks on the card, roughly measure the size of the design, including any repeating patterns. Keep the design away from the edges of the card. Dab or rub across the stencil lightly with ink, applying the colour as drily as possible. Repeat the application, if necessary, to achieve the depth of colour you require.

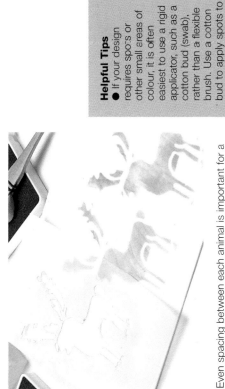

3 Even spacing between each animal is important for a professional look. Likewise, the pressure and depth of colour on each reindeer should also be similar, unless you wish to make them totally different colours.

Helpful Tips
- If your design requires spots or other small areas of colour, it is often easiest to use a rigid applicator, such as a cotton bud (swab), rather than a flexible brush. Use a cotton bud to apply spots to animals, balloons or other features.

4 Once the reindeer are painted, and you are happy with the colour, paint in the eyes. Rub a cotton bud on to the ink pad, erring on the side of caution with the amount of colour. Dab in the reindeer eyes with the cotton bud.

5 Complete all the reindeers' eyes. Finally, apply red to Rudolph's nose (the reindeer at the right of the design). All the animals could be given red noses, if you like, or paint black noses on the remaining reindeer.

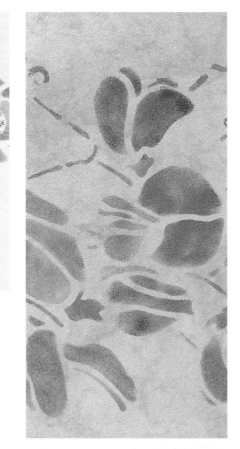

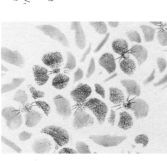

Helpful Tips

● A successful method of stencilling on cards is to apply the colour with a sponge. Sponge applicators are easy to control, making them particularly suitable for painting detailed areas. A small sponge can be used equally well; it should be rubbed over the ink pad and then dabbed evenly over the area to be coloured.

ABOVE This card would be ideal for a wedding or anniversary. The bell has been sponged with several colours to give an unusual golden yellow and brown effect, and the bow and flowers can be coloured to suit the occasion – for example, you may like to colour the ribbons gold for a golden wedding anniversary card.

RIGHT Pansies must rate as one of the world's favourite flowers, after the rose. These little heartsease pansies are stencilled in shades of purple and yellow, and would be a safe choice for any friend or relative.

BELOW The delicate shades of sweet peas offer plenty of inspiration for choosing colours. As these sweet peas have been stencilled on to a green card, stronger colours have been chosen to make sure they stand out. If you use a white or cream card, then paler colours would be equally successful.

OPPOSITE This selection of cards shows only a very small number of the many possible designs you could create. Handmade cards are unique and lend an extra-special touch to all occasions and celebrations.

LEFT Bright anemones make a perfect design for a cheering get-well card. There are many vivid colours in the anemone palette that could be used. Here, blue and pink make a striking effect and the black centres stand out strongly.

Memories of the Sea

Decorating Photograph Frames and Mounts

Often photographs lie in an album ignored for years, but if you display your favourite pictures from this year's holiday in a beautiful frame, like the one shown here, they can be admired long after the special event. You easily change the photographs after your next holiday to update the collection. Of course, the techniques used here can be adapted to produce a frame and mount for any other photographic subject, such as using tiny heart and flower stencils to frame snapshots of children.

Multi-aperture mounts are usually available from craft shops and photography sections in department stores as part of a standard collection. However, the spacing between the openings is usually much tighter than the mount of a standard collection. If you are using a mount with narrow spaces, you will need to use a tiny, delicate design and stencilling around these areas is actually much more difficult than it might seem. A mount with wider spaces can be cut to your requirements by a specialist picture-framing establishment.

Plain, wide frames are fairly easy to find. A specialist picture framer may be able to help you, but look in large chain stores because a standard range of frames may provide something suitable for this

project. The frame should be as wide, plain and flat as possible and made of unfinished wood. Many frames have decorative mouldings which make adding a stencil design difficult. A frame without woodwork details is simple to stencil on, and unfinished wood takes colour well and can be varnished to protect the design. You can sand down a glossy frame, but if the frame is too highly polished or is plastic, this may not be a viable option.

Several coats of varnish must be applied to the frame after stencilling, to protect the design from damage and so you can handle the frame as much as you like to change the photographs inside. If you want to hang the frame on the wall, you will need two screw eyes to secure to the frame so you can attach wire or string across the back. If you want to stand the frame up on a table, you will need a back for the picture with a free-standing strut.

Stencilled frames and mounts also make delightful gifts. You may like to give one of your own creations as a present for someone's birthday, and include cake, candles and party hats as stencil motifs along with photographs from previous birthdays. Even special awards or academic degrees can be commemorated in a decorative frame.

Materials

- Plain, wide, unvarnished wooden photo frame
- Mount board with several apertures to fit the frame
- Photographs
- Seaside stencils (see Stencil Templates, pages 103)
- Oil-based stencilling sticks or water-based ink stamping pads in blue, purple, red and green, or colours of your choice
- Size 2 and 4 stencilling brushes, or sponges
- Glass palette
- Satin or matt aerosol spray varnish

1 Make sure you have suitably sized brushes, or enough sponges, for each colour of paint you intend to use. Carefully plan where you want your decoration to go before you commit paint to wood or mount board. The designs should be planned so they are evenly spaced out.

2 Decorate the frame first with your largest stencils, such as the boats and lighthouse used here.

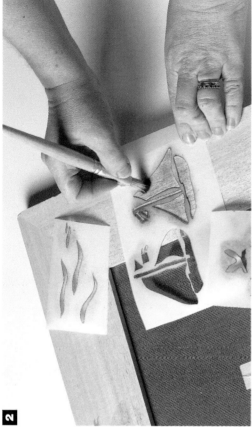

3 Intersperse delicate details among the heavier motifs. Here, a few birds lighten the frame and fill in spaces. When you have finished, put the frame on one side to dry and start work on the mount board.

Helpful Tips

● When you buy or cut the mount board for the frame, make sure that the holes are cut far enough apart to leave plenty of room for your stencilled designs. To cut your own holes, trace appropriate squares or rectangles on the board (circles are difficult to execute and are best avoided). Using a scalpel, metal ruler and a cutting mat, carefully cut out each shape. Cut in a smooth long line with the blade against the ruler. For a bevelled edge, angle the blade at about 80°.

4

4 The mount can be stencilled with designs matching the frame or with complementary motifs, as shown here. The marine theme is carried through from the frame to the mount with soft colours.

BELOW The base of the frame is given weight by some buildings which are painted in cheerful colours. Many other features could be included, for example trees, flowers or beach umbrellas.

ABOVE Do not use very bright colours on the mount or the photographs will be overwhelmed and will not look their best.

BELOW The stencilled motifs can be painted in any colour scheme. Here the blue marine theme has been changed to a bright sunny colour scheme, highlighted in yellow and brown.

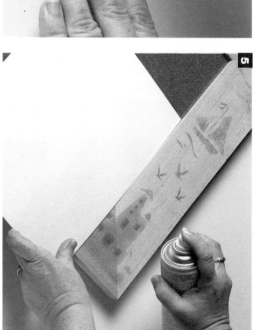

5 Once the frame is dry, spray it well with varnish because it will be handled quite extensively and the varnish will protect the paint effects. The mount, however, does not need to be sprayed because it will be protected behind the glass.

5

Helpful Tips

● Small pieces of natural or synthetic sponge can also be used as applicators. Because you are working on narrow areas with fairly small stencils, the sponges can be cut to a size that is manageable for you. The colour is dabbed on with the sponge – a useful method for creating soft colouring.

OPPOSITE Seaside motifs in soft colours add fun to this plain wooden frame. To add interest, you could also paint the frame a pale colour before decorating.

Garden Flowers

Creating Stylish Cushion Covers

C ushion or pillow covers can be decorated so easily with a simple stencil and a selection of fabric paints. Fabric paints are absolutely essential, as the standard acrylic, watercolour or other paints may run and smudge on the fabric. More importantly, fabric paints will enable your finished item to be laundered, which in the case of cushion covers is essential. For more on fabric paints, see pages 10 and 84.

Plain cotton or calico (muslin) cushion covers are inexpensive to buy, yet become beautiful hand-painted creations with a little artistic input. Any plain covers can be decorated; the ones used here are unbleached calico that has been piped with some coloured cotton fabric, but you may prefer to use another type of fabric. A relatively smooth fabric, rather than one with too coarse or textured a weave, is easiest to stencil on. You will also find a patterned fabric virtually impossible to stencil successfully, and chintzes or other glazed fabrics are not suitable for this method of decorating. If you feel so inclined, make your own cushions following one of the many patterns available from department stores and sewing shops. You will need to make sure your fabrics are colour-fast and preshrunk before you begin sewing and stencilling.

The paint effect will withstand machine-washing, but only occasionally, and it is not intended to be subjected to really heavy wear.

There are so many different fabric items that lend themselves to stencilled decoration. With original stencil designs and careful planning, you can create a range of household items that are completely unique and add a new dimension to any room. Often the size of the budget allocated to redecorate a room is not the key to success, and some creative thought and unusual decorative ideas can give a much more satisfactory result.

The technique used in this project can also be used for pillows, linen, duvet covers and throws for beds or sofas. Once you have become proficient with fabric stencilling, the possible projects are endless. However, any heavily-used linen that is going to be washed every week would not be suitable for stencilled decoration. A better option is to use undecorated sheets and pillowcases, and display a hand-stencilled bedspread on top of the bed. Or, place a selection of pretty pastel pillows on the bed that are for ornamental use only. If the pillows are small enough and the colours work together well, you can use a great variety of different paint effects and designs.

Materials
- Plain, cotton or calico (muslin) cushion covers
- Honeysuckle or other floral stencils
- Fabric paints in yellow ochre, maroon and green, or colours of your choice
- Size 2 and 4 stencilling brushes
- Glass palette

2 Stencil on the first colour. Here a yellow ochre was used for the honeysuckle stencil. Either shade a lighter colour into the centre, or use the second colour you have chosen, such as the maroon shown here.

3 Add the second colour on to the flowers. Some could be completely maroon, and some shaded yellow and maroon. More than two colours could be used for the flowers if you like; for example, a pale pink or peach colour could be introduced here.

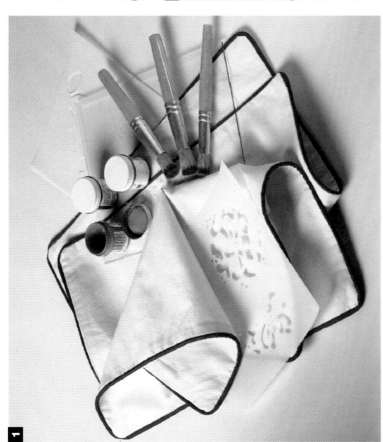

1 Wash the cushion cover first to ensure that it is clean and preshrunk, and make sure you have suitably sized brushes for each colour you will use. This design is a random pattern, so needs little measuring, but if you choose a geometric pattern, then careful thought and planning should go into the positioning of the stencils.

4 Next add the leaves and stems, twisting them across the cushion. With a naturally trailing design like this honeysuckle here, it is simple to do a randomly spaced pattern.

5 Once you have complete the cushion, the fabric paints must be fixed (set) with an iron. Read the instructions that accompany the fabric paints, because the technique may vary from one manufacturer to another.

Helpful Tips

● If this is your first attempt at using fabric paints, practice on a spare piece of fabric first to make sure you get a feeling for using the paints. Always use less paint than you think necessary and add a little more later to darken the colour.

OPPOSITE Wisteria, iris and lily designs are painted on these delightful cushions in fabric paints. Before starting, plan your design by choosing a colour scheme or design to suit your interior decoration.

LEFT This pretty wisteria design would look lovely in a bedroom or living room. The same design could be used on the walls to create a complete theme for a room, especially if you have wisteria climbing outside one of the windows.

LEFT Choose the colour scheme that will blend well with the room in which you intend to use your newly stencilled cushion. You could pick out one main colour from a sofa or curtain fabric, or just scatter a range of pretty designs across a bed or chair.

Golden Lilies

Stencilling a Small Tablecloth

This tablecloth shows how an inexpensive fabric, in this case plain calico (muslin), can be transformed into an object of beauty. The small size of this cloth is ideal for a bedside table or circular occasional table that has just enough space for a reading lamp or ornament, but you can decorate any size of tablecloth by following the techniques shown here. A special table is not necessary because it will not be visible beneath the cloth, and chipboard tables that are sold as flat packs and which slot together easily are ideal. Although the chipboard tables are pretty unattractive when uncovered, you are unaware of the furniture once the cloth is in place.

If you cannot find a plain calico tablecloth, there are many plain cotton cloths available in all shapes and sizes, and a coloured background might work better with your colour scheme. For example, the lily design shown here could be used on a pale gold, primrose yellow or even a very pale green fabric, and a wisteria design on a pale lilac or mauve background can look absolutely wonderful. Dark backgrounds are very difficult to use successfully, apart from such notable exceptions as gold stars on a navy or black background. A more cost-effective alternative is to make your own tablecloth from a simple

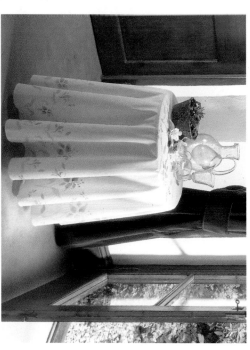

hemmed square of fabric. The extra benefit in making your own tablecloth is that you can add a trim or edging to the cloth that reflects the stencil decoration or emphasizes one of the colours you have used. If you are skilled at sewing, you could even create a scalloped or other decorative hem to the cloth that follows the pattern of the stencilled border.

Fabric paints are necessary for this project and they are available in a fairly wide range of colours. The colours show up on the fabric much the same as they appear in the pot, which makes choosing the paints to match your colour scheme quite easy. The colours can be strengthened by painting over a stencil several

times and you can mix the paints to gain new colours; the colours also mix together well when you use one on top of another.

If you do not want to use a floral design, then there are plenty of other possibilities. Do bear in mind the extra bonus when using floral designs: if you have a small space that is not large enough to take a full flower or repeat, you can add odd leaves, stalks or buds without spoiling the overall effect. This really does make life easier, as exact repeats of a geometric design have a habit of not quite fitting, even though you have carefully measured the item to be stencilled.

Golden Lilies

Materials
- Plain cotton or calico (muslin) circular tablecloth
- Lily or other floral stencils
- Fabric paints in green, yellow and ochre, or colours of your choice
- Size 4 and 6 stencilling brushes
- Glass palette

1 Wash the tablecloth first, and make sure you have suitably sized brushes for each colour. This design is an ordered composition and will need planning to ensure that the stencils are evenly spaced.

You can measure the cloth by dividing it into equal segments and marking where the lilies should be placed. To decorate the middle, simply fold the cloth in half, then in half again, to locate the exact centre.

2 Apply green fabric paint to the leaf section of the lily stencil, following your marked positions so the flowers are carefully and exactly spaced all around the edge of the tablecloth.

3 Next add a pale colour, such as the yellow shown here, for the outside of the petals. This can be shaded towards the centre of the flower if you wish. The lilies can either be all the same colour or a selection of different colours can be introduced.

4

4 Then add the darker, ochre, colour in the centre of the flower as shading. This adds depth and interest to the design and helps create a more professional look.

5 Once you have painted your decoration all the way around the base of the cloth and the paints are dry, the design must be fixed (set). Read the instructions that accompany the paints and iron both sides of the cloth to make the design washable.

5

Helpful Tips
● It is much easier to stencil a design in the centre of a tablecloth when the cloth is in position on the table. Do remember to place thick paper or cardboard under the cloth to protect the table from any paint that may seep through.

OPPOSITE This charming table cloth is decorated in the centre as well as along the edge. If you intend to display items on the table, it is a good idea to protect the cloth with a sheet of glass cut to the size of the table.

LEFT Decorate only the edges of the cloth if you intend to display something on the table that may damage the paintwork. Otherwise, you can stencil a design around a smaller circular area in the centre of the cloth.

LEFT For a simple design, stencil only one type of lily around the edge. For a more complex decoration, use smaller lilies and buds, plus a bee or butterfly to expand the design.

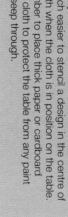

Kitchen Flowers

Matching Motifs on Kitchen Accessories

There are many utilitarian kitchen items that can be given a special look with a simple stencil or two. Oven gloves or mitts are not very glamorous pieces, but they are a useful and necessary cooking aid. In this project, several varieties of oven gloves and pads have been made from calico (muslin) and decorated with various floral motifs. Although these items are very simple to make from fabric if you like to sew, plain cotton versions can be purchased and decorated in the same way.

A coordinated set of items for the kitchen looks lovely and makes a wonderful gift. You could give a selection of oven gloves, hot pads, place mats, napkins and even an apron as a present. If you enjoy sewing, you may like to make a pad on which to rest hot plates and fill it with herbs and spices so that the aroma is released as the pad is warmed. Whatever item you choose to stencil, keep in mind that the decorated items can not be washed frequently.

As these are kitchen items, you might like to use a food theme for your design, such as vegetables or fruit. Many people have a cow, pig or other animal theme in the kitchen, and these shapes work really well as stencils and could be repeated on the walls. Other kitchen

holding the blind back, I suggest you stretch the blind out on a large table or the floor and weigh the corners down with tin cans or weights from a kitchen scale. This way you will have a firm, flat surface area to work on. Choose themes for your decoration that tie in with your kitchen. Often brighter, bolder patterns look more attractive than dainty designs on blinds. Remember that only part of the decoration will be seen at times, so check that the design looks attractive if only the bottom few inches are showing. Make sure that you do not stencil the design upside down and that you work from top to bottom.

accessories can be stencilled too, and toaster or appliance covers look great with a little added colour stencilled on. Decorated tea towels or cloths for trays could add a special individual touch to your kitchen, provided they are reserved for limited use.

One of the most striking items to stencil in a kitchen is a roller blind. Roller blinds are completely flat and therefore present no problems in adding a stencilled design. The only knack is getting them to stay open so you can work on them, assuming that you are decorating a ready-made blind rather than using a special kit. Having struggled with two members of my family

1 Make sure the oven gloves and pads are clean, and that you have the right brushes for each colour you will use. The ivy design is a random pattern, so no planning is needed; however, if you choose a more elaborate stencil you may like to mark where the stencils will be positioned.

Materials
● Plain cotton or calico (muslin) oven gloves or mitts, or hot pads
● Ivy stencil (see Stencil Templates page 103), or any flower stencils of your choice
● Fabric paints in yellow ochre and green, or colours of your choice
● Size 2 and 4 stencilling brushes
● Glass palette

2 Apply the first colour on to your chosen accessory; here green fabric paint is used. You may find it helps to practice on a spare piece of cloth to find the right amount of paint and pressure to use.

3 Add the shading to the leaves. In this case, a yellow ochre was added to tone down the green and add some variation to the design. Obviously, many other colourways would be equally successful.

89

4 Once you are happy with the design and the paint is dry, read any instructions that accompany your fabric paints. Then iron both sides of the glove or mitt to fix (set) the paint.

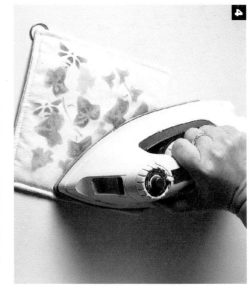

BELOW If you are using a simple design with a minimal number of colours, make sure that enough visual interest is apparent in the design. Details, such as the bee added to this hot pad, can turn a sparse design into something more stunning.

OPPOSITE A range of plain kitchen mitts and hot pads can be given your own individual style with the simple addition of a few stencil motifs.

ABOVE These plain oven mitts have simple daisies stencilled on to them. Other kitchen accessories can be decorated, such as tea towels and egg cosies.

ABOVE These oven gloves are decorated with a design that lends itself to the long shape. Alternatively, you could decorate them with a border all around the edge of the gloves and add a few flowers in the middle.

Helpful Tips
● Although fabric paints are available in a very wide range of colours, it is also possible to create colours by placing a small sample of each colour on to your glass palette and mixing them.

Butterflies and Bees

Using Delicate Designs on Voile Curtains

N et or voile curtains are sometimes necessary, particularly if you have a room that overlooks a street. Plain nets can be a little dull, and frilly nets do not always match your style of decor. This project adds an unusual decorative touch to a window, while keeping the privacy that voile curtains can offer.

Voile is available in cream or white and the choice of colour is yours. Always consider the other colours or items in the room. White tends to look more modern, while cream has an older, more antique, look. A simple hem on each end is all that is required, because the curtains can hang on a curtain wire or rod.

Fabric paints are the ideal medium to use on this project, but if you are particularly keen to match the colours used elsewhere in the room, then the oil-based stencilling sticks can be used. Although the curtains will not be washable if you use the sticks, the paints do give a good strong colour. Fabric paints, though, are absolutely necessary if your curtains need frequent washing. The best method for applying colour to a large piece of fabric is to work on a protected tabletop with chairs at one end to drape the fabric over as you work. You can then simply push the fabric along and the paint can dry without danger of smudging.

the curtain with taller flowers, like hollyhocks or delphiniums, rising up the curtain. Trailing ivy looks very effective and a dramatic design could be achieved by stencilling a hanging basket on to the curtain to give a kind of trompe-l'oeil effect.

Traditional curtains can also be decorated with stencils, but as they are usually drawn back, the best design is a border along the edges or a random pattern all over the curtain. Wooden shutters look stunning when decorated with a stencil design and these make an attractive alternative to curtains.

The amount of stencilling you want to add to the curtains is up to you. If you just want to add a pretty touch here and there, a light scattering of butterflies and bees, as in the project shown here, would be sufficient. If you want to make the curtains considerably darker, a heavily stencilled pattern that covers a fair percentage of the curtain is the best choice for you.

There are so many other designs that would work equally well with this fabric. Keeping the airy feel to the design, you could stencil bluebirds, stars, moons or suns on to the curtains. Or you could add a garden theme to the room with a border of flowers along the bottom of

Materials

- Voile curtains
- Butterfly, bee or other insect stencils
- Fabric paints or oil-based stencilling sticks in light blue, dark blue and gold, or colours of your choice
- Size 2 and 4 stencilling brushes
- Glass palette

1 Begin by washing your curtains so they are clean and preshrunk. Make sure you have suitably sized brushes for each colour you will use. The butterfly and bee motifs create a random pattern all over the curtain, so no advance planning is necessary.

2 Starting from either the top or bottom of the curtain, depending on your preference, stencil a random collection of bees across the fabric. Here the bees have been stencilled with a bright gold paint for impact.

3 These butterflies are created with a two-part stencil. First randomly stencil the butterflies all over the fabric with the paler blue colour. It is essential to use a lighter colour first and then shade with a darker colour, as the reverse is not successful.

Helpful Tips

● Other fabrics can be used to produce this beautiful curtain, such as muslin (gauze muslin), lightweight calico (muslin lining), netting, or any other fabric that allows the light to shine through.

4 Add the darker blue shading in the centre of the butterfly. Alternatively, you could use gold again in the middle of some butterflies and the dark blue for the rest.

5 Once the decoration is complete, read the manufacturer's instructions that accompany the fabric paints and carefully iron the curtains on both sides to fix (set) the design.

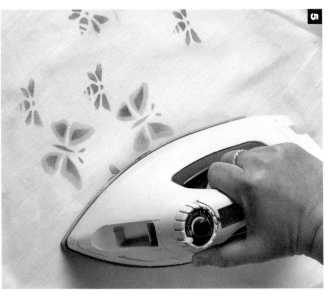

9 4

ABOVE A random selection of insects looks more impressive than a regimented pattern for a delicate curtain such as this one. Other small stencils, such as tiny flowers and buds, fleur-de-lis and gold stars, could look equally impressive. You may even want to experiment with a white-on-white effect, using white or cream fabric paints for a very subtle decoration.

OPPOSITE A sprinkling of blue butterflies and gold bees lightly decorate this plain voile curtain. Soft and metallic colours enhance the effect natural light makes when it shines through the curtain.

Floral Features

Embellishing Plain Curtain Tie-backs

Plain curtain tie-backs can be made at home, if you are handy with a needle and thread, or plain cotton or calico (muslin) versions can be purchased and then decorated. Because the tie-backs are wrapped around the curtains to hold them back, you will need to attach plain or decorative cup-hooks into the wall at the appropriate positions so the ties can be secured.

Fabric paints are necessary for this project, as it is convenient to be able to wash the tie-backs. If you would prefer to use other paints, use the oil-based stencil sticks, but remember that the finished tie-backs can not be washed. Whether this is a major problem for you or not depends on how rigorously you carry out your cleaning routine and how much the tie-backs would be used. If the tie-backs are only hanging decoratively in a spare bedroom and will not be subjected to dust and dirt, you might choose to use the same paints you have used on the walls so the colours match exactly.

Although the design shown here is a fairly simple one, the amount of space to stencil on the tie-back is somewhat limited. Even the broadest tie-backs will need a fairly dainty stencil design that is small and uncomplicated enough to fit comfortably into the space allowed.

Curtain pelmets can also be stencilled, whether they are constructed from hardboard or wood and painted with several coats of emulsion paint, or made from plain fabric, such as cotton or calico. A hardboard pelmet can be cut with a jigsaw along the edge to match the outline of your stencil, and this makes a highly ornamental and unusual feature in the room. Stencilled pelmets and tie-backs look impressive when used with plain curtains, but you may prefer to decorate all elements, depending on the complexity of your design and the effect you want to achieve.

If the tie-backs are to be used with heavily stencilled curtains, then just a spray of leaves, a posy of flowers, or a butterfly or two will be sufficient.

You may like to make curtains to match your tie-backs (see pages 92–5), and you can use either the same stencil design on both items or repeat a small detail from the curtain design on to the tie-backs. Another successful combination for home furnishings is to use plain-coloured curtains with tie-backs that are decorated with the same design as a stencilled border or random pattern on the walls. Plain curtains in a simple, solid colour make a good contrast to stencilled walls and tie-backs.

Materials

- Plain cotton or calico (muslin) tie-backs
- Floral stencils (see Stencil Templates, page 103)
- Fabric paints in pale green, pink and brown, or colours of your choice
- Size 2 and 4 stencilling brushes
- Glass palette

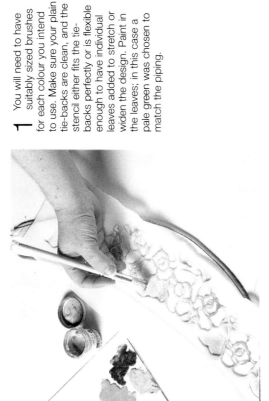

1 You will need to have suitably sized brushes for each colour you intend to use. Make sure your plain tie-backs are clean, and the stencil either fits the tie-backs perfectly or is flexible enough to have individual leaves added to stretch or widen the design. Paint in the leaves; in this case a pale green was chosen to match the piping.

2 Add a pale pink to the outer petals on the flowers. You could use a variety of colours if you wish, or just one pale pink and one darker pink for shading and contrast.

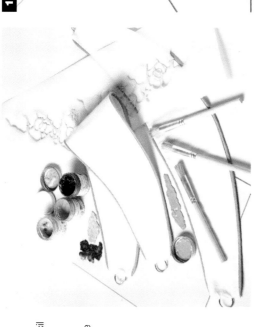

3 Add the darker colour in the centre and on a few of the edges of the flowers to give shading and detail to the design. A darker green could also be used to shade the leaves if you wished.

LEFT These blue roses look very striking and just as pretty as conventional reds, pinks or peach colours.

4 Iron the finished design carefully to fix (set) the fabric paints, following the manufacturer's instructions. Do make sure that the paint is dry first, as it is easy to smudge your design if you try to iron it too soon after stencilling.

5 Although it will barely be seen, it is a nice touch to decorate the back of the tie-back. This will be glimpsed when the curtains are closed and the tie-back hangs down unused. Begin with the leaves.

6 To finish the back of the tie-back, apply the pink paint to the flower, then shade with the brown colour. You could also use a simple spray of leaves or a couple of flowers for this detail.

Helpful Tips
● If you have a patterned curtain, copy a motif from the curtains to create a stencil for the tie-backs. Use one single colour taken from the colours of the curtain and you will have plain tie-backs with a stencilled motif that matches your curtain fabric.

OPPOSITE These eye-catching rose tie-backs look beautiful when set against plain curtains. The design gracefully fills the space on the tie-backs, but you could also use just one or two small simple rosebuds.

Index

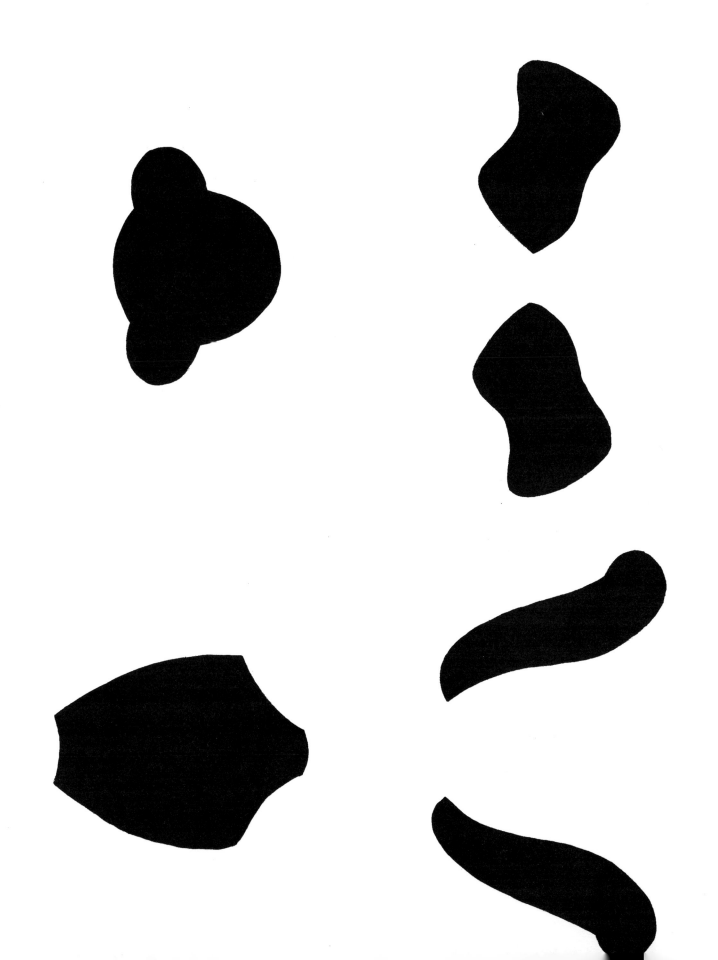